Policy Coherence for Development in the EU Council

Strategies for the Way Forward

Project Leader

Christian Egenhofer

Authors

Louise van Schaik
Michael Kaeding
Alan Hudson
Jorge Núñez Ferrer

With expert contributions by

Sergio Carrera
Meng-Hsuan Chou
David Kernohan
Andreas Schneider
Lorna Schrefler
Marius Vahl

CENTRE FOR EUROPEAN POLICY STUDIES
BRUSSELS

10247123

The Centre for European Policy Studies (CEPS) is an independent policy research institute based in Brussels. Its mission is to produce sound analytical research leading to constructive solutions to the challenges facing Europe today. The views expressed in this report are those of the authors writing in a personal capacity and do not necessarily reflect those of CEPS or any other institution with which the authors are associated.

ISBN 92-9079-653-7

Centre for European Policy Studies
Place du Congrès 1, B-1000 Brussels
Tel: 32 (0) 2 229.39.11 Fax: 32 (0) 2 219.41.51
e-mail: info@ceps.be
internet: http://www.ceps.be

CONTENTS

List of Figures

List of Tables

PREFACE

It is widely recognised that aid alone cannot solve the problems of development in poor countries. Many other policy areas have an impact on living standards and economic opportunities, and their formulation and implementation therefore need to be closely coordinated. This study aims to contribute to the growing debate on 'policy coherence for development' (PCD), a concept elaborated upon in the European Commission's April 2005 Communication on policy coherence for development – Accelerating progress towards attaining the Millennium Development Goals – and the Council Conclusions on policy coherence for development of May 2005. It is intended to complement other research in this field. The study was carried out by CEPS with financial support provided by the UK Department for International Development. CEPS would particularly like to thank the numerous officials and experts who were consulted or interviewed in the course of the study, DG Development of the European Commission for its cooperation, as well as members of the Committee on Development Cooperation (CODEV) and the informal PCD network. Nevertheless, the authors alone are responsible for its content.

I would like to extend particular thanks to all those both within and outside CEPS who contributed to this study and made it possible. My appreciation goes first to Michael Kaeding of both Leiden University and CEPS, who efficiently coordinated the project while also contributing to the empirical parts of the study (i.e. the sectoral fiches) as well as the analysis in Part I. Alan Hudson from the Overseas Development Institute (ODI) provided the heart of the development expertise and was the author of all six case studies. My CEPS colleague Louise van Schaik acted as lead author for the analytical and prescriptive sections in Part I and was also responsible for significant portions of the sectoral analyses in Part II. I would also like to mention the special contribution of Jorge Núñez Ferrer, also of CEPS, not only for his constructive comments on several versions of the report but also for his valuable input of key sections. Finally, this report would not have been possible without the additional contributions to the sectoral studies by several other CEPS research fellows, namely Sergio Carrera, Meng-Hsuan Chou, David Kernohan, Andreas Schneider, Lorna Schrefler and Marius Vahl.

Christian Egenhofer
Project Leader

Policy Coherence for Development in the EU Council:
Strategies for the Way Forward
A Special CEPS Report
Executive Summary

A id alone cannot meet the needs of the poor in developing countries. The European Union is increasingly aware that many of its policies outside of official development assistance have a decisive impact on those living in third world countries. In recognition of that fact, the EU has made policy coherence for development (PCD) a central pillar in its concerted efforts to realise the UN Millennium Development Goals.

This study focuses on the policy-making processes in the Council of the EU (sometimes also referred to as the Council of Ministers). Since EU policies are generally (co-)decided in the Council, this institution is of vital importance for ensuring policy coherence in general and PCD in particular. We analyse whether the policy-making processes in the EU Council allow for 'development-related' inputs and where these processes are found to be wanting, we put forth policy recommendations on how PCD could be strengthened. In addition, where relevant, the role of other institutions, notably the European Commission, is examined.

Studies were conducted in each of the 12 thematic areas identified in the May 2005 Council Conclusions on PCD: trade, environment, climate change, security, agriculture, fisheries, the social dimension of globalisation, employment and decent work, migration, research and innovation, the information society, transport and energy. For each of these policy areas, a 'fiche' has been prepared that describes in detail the EU policy-making process and how – if at all – development-related inputs are introduced into this process. An accompanying organigram diagrams the process and the relationship of the principal players. In addition, six in-depth case studies were carried out in the areas of agriculture, fisheries, trade, climate change, migration and security. The fiches and case studies can be found in Part II of this report.

Key findings

General observations

1. Policy coherence in general, and by extension, policy coherence for development, are easier to ensure in the policy-making processes in the European Commission than in the EU Council. The main reason is that decisions are ultimately taken by the Commission as a whole, thereby allowing all interests to be represented and cleared at the central level, i.e. the college of Commissioners, whereas decision-making in the Council must navigate the nine sectorally-divided ministerial formations and numerous subordinate bodies, where the majority of decisions are taken.

2. PCD depends on many factors, including which directorate-general (DG) in the European Commission assumes the lead in drafting proposals; which Council working party, Coreper and Council formation are in charge; and the extent to which the European Council, the EU presidency and the General Affairs and External Relations Council (GAERC) actively promote the consideration of development implications in the decision-making process.

Strengthening PCD in EU policy-making processes

A. Council of the European Union

3. *The European Council*, reinforced at times by the EU presidency, has played a significant role in promoting PCD. Of particular benefit to PCD is the fact that all ministerial Council formations can provide input, via the GAERC, to the preparatory groundwork for summits and the subsequent presidency conclusions. However, only a minority of issues is covered by the European Council.

4. Several *EU presidencies* have been instrumental in promoting PCD. The presidency chairs and sets the agenda of Council meetings and represents the EU Council vis-à-vis the other EU institutions and externally.

5. The study has identified the importance of *single member states* or coalitions of member states to advance the case of PCD at the EU level.

6. The *GAERC* is another important advocate for PCD, although its performance on PCD has been uneven. The more intensively the GAERC deals with policy coherence for development, the more

CODEV (Committee on Development Cooperation), as its preparatory body on these matters, is obliged to concentrate on PCD matters.

7. *Coreper* is very important for PCD, given that the work of the various sectoral working parties for most policy files comes together in this body, before being channelled up to the relevant Council formations. Coreper is in a key position as it not only prepares the decisions for the Council but it also can reach agreement itself by issuing 'A points', which are adopted at the ministerial level without further discussion. Nevertheless, our study indicates that Coreper has yet to realise its potential significance for policy coherence for development. Moreover, the division of labour between Coreper I and Coreper II poses further challenges in ensuring coherence.

B. European Commission

8. When non-development DGs are in the lead, it can be a challenge to ensure that the development implications of a proposal are properly understood and taken into account.

9. Legitimate concerns expressed by civil society, developing countries or other stakeholders in the course of consultations have not always been incorporated in the final decisions.

10. Inter-service consultation and integrated impact assessments on policy proposals are two crucial tools for bringing development concerns forward to DG Development, but to date these have been insufficiently employed.

11. Relevant cabinet members, supported by DG Development, and notably the Commissioner for Development, have a particular responsibility to promote PCD.

12. As the guardian of the treaties, the Commission is obliged to ensure that policy proposals respect EU laws and policy priorities, including PCD. Accordingly, within Council negotiations, the European Commission has the ability to advance the case for PCD.

Six proposals for structural reform

This study outlines six concrete proposals for reinforcing PCD in the decision-making processes in the EU Council, as follows:

1. Strengthen the accountability of ministers in the Council formations, including their stance on PCD and how EU PCD objectives are incorporated in EU policy, by requiring more explicit reporting to the

GAERC and more independent studies on development implications of decisions taken.

2. Strengthen existing expert groups and create several new ones to focus on the link between a particular sectoral policy and development. These PCD expert groups would report to both the sector-specific working party and to CODEV.

3. Appoint independent PCD observers to take part in the meetings of the senior preparatory committees, where sectoral interests are found to be particularly salient. The PCD observers would report to CODEV and Coreper II, and if appropriate to the GAERC.

4. Require periodic and public reporting by the Council Secretariat and its Legal Service to Coreper and the GAERC on the progress made in ensuring that relevant conclusions and decisions on PCD are respected, notably in non-development policies.

5. Significantly expand the capacity in DG Development and other DGs to ensure that development concerns are fully taken into account and are made explicit in Commission proposals in such a way that is understandable to non-development specialists as well.

6. Require all decisions taken by Comitology Committees[1] with external implications in the 12 policy areas identified in the May 2005 Council Conclusions on PCD to be reported to DG Development (European Commission) and the PCD expert groups.

Specific recommendations for improving the potential for PCD

Below we specify more specific recommendations, or courses of action for the Council of the EU and the European Commission. We further distinguish between immediate and longer-term action, acknowledging that the latter will require more complex structural changes.

---

[1] Comitology committees oversee the implementation of EU legislation and are made up primarily of national officials and experts, and chaired by the European Commission.

For immediate action

Council of the EU

1. The EU presidency should use its power for assigning files to the appropriate Council formation, irrespective of where the file has been handled in the European Commission (the study has shown that it matters for PCD which Council formation is responsible).

2. When PCD-related issues of significant political weight are at stake, the presidency should consider establishing a 'Friends of the Presidency group' to handle a file in a genuinely cross-cutting way.

3. The GAERC should better utilise its coordination role within the Council with regard to PCD and be actively engaged in all 12 policy areas listed in the Council Conclusions on PCD. It should particularly ensure that the bi-annual PCD Work Programme is of sufficient substance before adoption and ensure its implementation afterwards.

4. Council formations dealing with issues covered by the PCD Council conclusions should report periodically and publicly to the GAERC on how PCD has been taken into account in relevant decisions. For instance, these reports should coincide with GAERC discussions on the PCD Work Programme.

5. Coreper should pay more attention to PCD and ensure that the work between its two formations is better coordinated, for instance by introducing PCD as a standing concern in the Mertens and Antici Groups, which prepare the meetings of Coreper.

6. Even in cases where the senior Council preparatory committee has resolved most of the substantive points on a file, Coreper should still be in a position to review the file in the light of PCD.

7. Special PCD observers should be appointed to monitor the work of the senior preparatory committees, which have a particularly strong focus on sectoral interests.

8. PCD expert groups should be created to advise the sector-specific working parties and CODEV on the links between non-development and development policies.[2] In instances where expert groups are

---

[2] For example, 12 such groups could operate corresponding to the areas specified in the Council Conclusions. They already exist for trade (the trade and development expert group) and climate change (the developing countries expert

insufficiently involved, CODEV should report to Coreper II and if necessary, to the GAERC.

9. CODEV and DG Development should agree that the latter reports regularly (e.g. four times a year) to CODEV on policy proposals and on draft negotiating mandates in the making that are relevant for PCD.

10. The Council Secretariat should regularly and publicly report to the GAERC on its efforts to ensure the coherence of Council conclusions, and hence their consistency with the Council conclusions on PCD and other GAERC conclusions on the link between policies and development.

European Commission

11. The European Commission should offer specific training courses on development implications to improve capacity and skills to deal with the development implications of policy proposals and existing EU legislation.

12. Decisions of comitology committees with external implications, including all decisions affecting conditions for exporting to the EU's internal market, should be notified to DG Development and CODEV (or to the newly created Expert Groups on PCD.)

For the longer term

Council of the EU

13. European Council presidency conclusions should regularly reiterate the importance of PCD in order to give the concept sufficient political weight in EU decision-making. PCD should be discussed in the European Council at least once a year.

14. EU presidencies should give high priority to policy coherence in general, and to PCD in particular. They must ensure that PCD has a prominent place in the multi-annual strategic programmes that are developed by subsequent presidencies, sponsor presidency workshops devoted to PCD-related topics, include PCD concerns in their external

---

group). For some areas, the groups could be combined, for instance alongside the Council formations. They could all be labelled as PCD expert groups to give explicit visibility to their PCD function.

representation activities and use their agenda-setting power to ensure that development implications are taken into consideration.

15. Coalitions of member states interested in PCD should develop initiatives to promote PCD in EU policies. These initiatives could include position papers, conferences, workshops, studies and support of development NGOs that are active at the European level.

16. The EU presidency should actively seek the involvement of the informal network on PCD to facilitate regular contact among development experts to discuss PCD.

17. The GAERC should actively promote PCD during European Council preparations by ensuring that development implications have been made explicit and that those implications are taken into account in the deliberations.

18. Development ministers should be enlisted to provide more weight to PCD via their participation in more meetings of the GAERC, notably when trade and other external policies with development implications are concerned.

19. CODEV should devote sufficient time to PCD and actively emphasise the importance of PCD in dialogue with other Council bodies.

20. The Council Secretariat should give special attention to improving awareness and provide training for officials to deal with issues that cut across two or more sectors, such as PCD.

21. Regular rotation of staff in the Council Secretariat should also be motivated by increasing awareness and understanding of policy coherence, including policy coherence for development.

22. As accountability and stakeholder involvement can be expected to increase with scrutiny by the European Parliament, areas that are currently not subject to co-decision, such as agriculture and fisheries, should become so.

European Commission

23. DG Development in the European Commission should provide sufficient resources to monitor policy developments in non-development DGs and to strengthen input in development-relevant files where DG development is not in the lead.

24. DG Development should pay particular attention to ensure that there are a sufficient number of officials with adequate skills and authority responsible for monitoring policy developments in non-development

DGs and to participate in inter-service consultation and impact assessments.

25. DG Development should be more assertive in promoting the interests of PCD during the inter-service consultation, and not shy away from blocking proposals that ignore the development side. Such assertiveness is important to raise the awareness of PCD within all levels of the Commission.

26. DG Development should consider the Commission's Legal Service as an ally on PCD, in the context of its responsibility to verify the consistency of new proposals with existing EU legislation and the EU treaties.

27. DG Development should strive to make development aspects and possible impacts of all development-relevant policies more explicit in Commission proposals, and to do this in such a way that it is understandable to non-specialists as well.

28. The European Commission should also consider strengthening the capacity of non-development DGs to ensure that policy coherence and by extension PCD is taken into account. Capacity and awareness will depend on the number, seniority and skill level of the officials tasked with policy coherence or PCD.

29. The Commission should incorporate development criteria in the Extended Impact Assessments of development-relevant policy proposals, as well as in other policy impact assessments and evaluations. DG Development should establish such criteria in close cooperation with other DGs.

30. The Commissioner for Development, supported by his or her cabinet and DG Development, should emphasise the development aspects of proposals where DG Development has not been in the lead, as these impacts are not always considered automatically by other Commissioners.

31. The Commission should promote PCD in a more pro-active manner in EU Council negotiations.

PART I. MAIN REPORT

1. Introduction

Progress in achieving the Millennium Development Goals (MDGs) in developing countries is not only determined by development cooperation policies, which tend to be centred on official development assistance (ODA), but also by policies implemented in other areas, such as agriculture, trade and migration. Initiatives in these latter fields can have a profound impact on living standards in poor countries, but they often work at cross-purposes. In recognition of this fact, the European Union, the governments of its member states and a number of international institutions, such as the OECD (Organisation for Economic Cooperation and Development), have affirmed 'policy coherence for development' (PCD) as an important principle for achieving more effective development cooperation.

Initial work in this area has mainly concentrated on ensuring consistency across policies within one single country (intra-governmental coherence) or on efforts in one particular area by a number of different countries (inter-governmental coherence). Hardly any attention has been paid to 'multilateral' coherence for development, especially at the EU level and in the EU Council in particular.

In 2005, the EU and its member states provided 53% of all official international development assistance.[1] Aside from the magnitude of its assistance to poor countries, there are other reasons why the EU, and notably the EU level of governance, is important for policy coherence for development. Many of the policies affecting development objectives are developed, formulated and finally decided at EU level. The provisions of the EC Treaty are directly applicable in all member states, and Community law takes precedence over national law. Moreover, the EU is an important

---

[1] The share of the EU 15 member states, all of which are also OECD members, is $55.7 billion. In addition, the Czech Republic, Poland and Slovakia have reported a total of $470 million in ODA to the OECD Development Assistance Committee (DAC). With total ODA figures in 2005 of $106.5 billion, this brings the EU's share to about 53% (see http://www.oecd.org/ document/40/0,2340,en_2649_34485_36418344_1_1_1_1,00.html).

player internationally, both for development cooperation and for its role in international fora, e.g. in the WTO or climate change negotiations.

This project breaks new ground as it investigates how policy-making processes in the EU Council influence PCD. Since EU policies are generally (co-)decided in the Council, this institution can play an important role in ensuring policy coherence in general and PCD in particular. In addition, where appropriate, the influence of notably the European Commission is taken into account as it initiates most policies decided upon in the Council and is an important participant in its meetings. The study also acknowledges the importance of the European Parliament and the member states, but as these institutions were outside the terms of reference, we only refer to other literature or specific examples of the contribution of these actors to PCD efforts.

The objective of this study is to examine whether policy-making processes in non-development policy areas accommodate 'development-related' inputs, thereby ensuring that these policies in these areas do not undermine development objectives. The aim is to identify concrete ways to enhance PCD. The analysis concentrates on 12 thematic areas identified in the May 2005 Council Conclusions on policy coherence for development: trade, environment, climate change, security, agriculture, fisheries, social dimension of globalisation, employment and decent work, migration, research and innovation, information society, transport and energy.

This study presents a 'fiche' for each of these 12 policy areas, describing in detail the EU policy-making process and how – if at all – development-related inputs are introduced into this process. In addition, in-depth case studies provide further analysis of specific policy-making processes in six of the 12 policy areas: agriculture, fisheries, trade, climate change, migration and security. The geographical focus of the case studies is sub-Saharan Africa, where over 40% of the population is still living below the poverty line and whose share of world trade diminished from 4% in 1987 to less than 2% in 2001 (OECD, 2003: 2). The information contained in both the fiches and the case studies is drawn from a review of the literature; face-to-face and telephone interviews with representatives from the member states participating in the EU Council bodies, Council Secretariat staff members and European Commission officials; as well as consultations with the 'informal PCD network', an informal forum to share ideas and analysis on PCD.[2] The fiches and case studies can be found in Part II of this study.

The remainder of this report is structured as follows: section 2 outlines the main studies and international initiatives undertaken on policy coherence for development and section 3 sets out the principal EU initiatives taken so far. Section 4 discusses how interests, including development interests, are balanced in the EU institutions and introduces the analytical distinction between Commission-led and member state-led policies. Section 5 analyses decision-making processes in the Council and the European Commission. Section 6 subsequently identifies key drivers for change, and section 7 concludes with a strategy for improving PCD and recommendations.

2.   The Context of Policy Coherence for Development

Interest in PCD has grown since the mid-1990s, notably as a result of globalisation and the expansion of the development agenda. Alongside traditional objectives, such as promoting economic development and meeting basic social needs, other goals relating to governance, democracy, respect for human rights, gender equality and environmental sustainability became part of development cooperation. In 2000, the United Nations agreed on a set of Millennium Development Goals (MDGs) aimed at alleviating poverty, illiteracy, hunger, discrimination against women, unsafe drinking water and a degraded environment, among others.[3] Subsequently, the Doha Development Agenda for trade launched in November 2001, the Monterrey Consensus on development financing established in March 2002 and the World Summit on Sustainable Development held in August 2002 provided additional initiatives for

---

[2] Established in 2003, the informal PCD network is open to all EU member states and the Commission. It is not intended to provide a parallel structure to the Council's Working Party on Development Cooperation (CODEV) nor does it have any formal decision-making power.

[3] The eight MDGs are to eradicate extreme poverty and hunger; achieve universal primary education; promote gender equality and empower women; reduce the mortality rate of children; improve maternal health; combat HIV/AIDS, malaria and other diseases; ensure environmental sustainability and develop a global partnership for development.

dialogue and renewed impetus to achieve policy coherence for development.

The OECD has been especially concerned with PCD. Its Development Assistance Committee (DAC), which includes most EU member states[4] and the European Community, has held donor countries responsible for ensuring a systematic promotion of mutually-reinforcing policy actions across government departments and agencies creating synergies towards achieving development objectives. The DAC Guidelines on Poverty Reduction state that "we should aim for nothing less than to assure that the entire range of relevant industrialized country policies are consistent with and do not undermine development objectives" (OECD, 2001: 90). These guidelines also contain a detailed section entitled "Towards Policy Coherence for Poverty Reduction".

In 2003, the OECD published a policy brief, which signalled a renewed effort to improve policy coherence for development in OECD countries. In 2005, it collected several OECD governments' experiences in enhancing policy coherence for poverty reduction (OECD, 2005a) and launched a new publication series, called 'The Development Dimension', which analyses the development aspects of non-development policies ranging from macroeconomic policy to migration (OECD, 2005b-h).

Within the EU, several member states have also undertaken special efforts: the UK published two White Papers on Eliminating World Poverty (DFID, 1997 & 2000); the Netherlands focused on 'de-compartmentalisation' to create synergies within and across all parts of the government; and a German ministerial regulation aimed at ensuring the systematic examination of all new legislation for its coherence with development policy.

Three other studies are worth mentioning. Ashoff's (2005) study *Enhancing Policy Coherence for Development: Justification, Recognition and Approaches to Achievement*, commissioned by the German Ministry for Economic Cooperation and Development, should be seen as a complement to the OECD 2005 report. It considers the justification for, the recognition and scope of and the limits to the goal of enhancing policy coherence for development. It focuses exclusively on national experiences in selected EU member states (the UK, Germany, the Netherlands and Sweden). Ashoff

---

[4] All EU15 member states belong to the DAC, but it does not include the 10 new member states that joined in 2004.

argues that PCD is a complex management task that is subject to constraints (e.g. a shortage of staff in ministries). He underlines the importance of political will and leadership, arguing that progress towards PCD depends to a considerable extent on the political weight and the commitment of the members of cabinet responsible for development cooperation. The study calls explicitly for increased international cooperation on the issue of PCD, for instance in the context of the G-8, the UN, the OECD as well as the EU Council.

A study by Hoebink (2005), entitled "The Coherence of EU Policies: Perspectives from the North and the South", focuses on the effects of existing EU policies, in particular in two countries, Morocco and Senegal. It discusses in detail the concept of policy coherence for development and the policies most related to it and suggests inter alia that the European Commission should pay more attention to PCD in the next generation of Country Strategy papers it produces.[5]

Yet another study on PCD was carried out by the European Centre for Development Policy Management and the Instituto Complutense de Estudios Internacionales (ECDPM & ICEI, 2005), entitled *EU mechanisms that promote policy coherence for development*. While it devotes a chapter to the European institutions along with others about the member state's efforts in policy coherence, it tries to reduce complexity by collapsing the European Commission, the Council of the EU and the European Parliament into one unitary actor. Such treatment does not fully capture the reality that the three European institutions have different legislative and executive powers and that the institutional balance between them differs from one policy field to another, depending on the extent of EU competencies and the decision-making procedure that applies.

The ECDPM is currently carrying out a follow-up study analysing in more detail specific mechanisms to promote policy coherence at the member state level. Sponsored by the French Ministry of Foreign Affairs, the study is part of an evaluation process conducted by the Heads of External Assistance Evaluation Services of the EU member states and is one

---

[5] The study was part of the European Union's Poverty Reduction Effectiveness Programme (PREP). For further information, visit the website http://www.ec-prep.org.

of the six joint studies monitored by this group. The study is due to be completed in the second half of 2006.

3. A Brief History of PCD in the EU

In early 1990s, development policy was incorporated in the EU Treaty at Maastricht in 1992, which entered into force in 1993. The Maastricht Treaty introduced the principles of coherence, coordination and complementarity (the '3 Cs') as the basis for the Treaty's application (Hoebink, 1999). In particular, Art. 178 of the EC Treaty stipulates that "the Community shall take account of the objectives referred to in Art. 177 (on development cooperation) in the policies that it implements which are likely to affect developing countries".

In 2003, the Netherlands took the initiative to establish a PCD network. In 2005 – in the light of the mid-term review of the MDGs – PCD was firmly established on the EU agenda. On 12 April 2005, the Commission adopted three Communications on the MDGs, one of which focused entirely on PCD.[6] With this Communication, the Commission made an important step forward as it looked beyond the borders of development cooperation centred on ODA. The Communication identifies policy areas where there is a large potential to achieve synergies among various development policy objectives. For each of these policy areas the Communication proposed 'PCD Commitments' and a series of specific actions intended to contribute to accelerating progress towards the MDGs.

On 24 May 2005, the EU Council in its General Affairs and External Relations formation, after a long and intensive debate, followed the Commission's new development approach and adopted ground-breaking Council Conclusions on policy coherence for development.[7] The Conclusions stipulated that the "Council will assess existing internal procedures, mechanisms and instruments to strengthen the effective

---

[6] The other parts of the package aimed at accelerating progress towards the MDGs by increasing the volume and effectiveness of the development aid provided by the European Commission and member states and by making more explicit the focus on the Least Developing Countries in Africa.

[7] It decided to focus on three main issues in EU development cooperation: 1) increasing the quantity and quality of development finance, 2) strengthening policy coherence for development and associating non-aid policies with the MDG agenda and 3) expending extra efforts in support of Africa.

integration of development concerns in its decision-making procedures on non-development policies". The Ministers in particular agreed 12 policy areas needing particular attention in terms of PCD, recognising the importance of non-development policies for assisting developing countries in achieving the MDGs. The policy-making process in these areas are analysed in Part II of this study.

In December 2005, the Council, the European Commission and the European Parliament jointly adopted the so-called 'European Consensus on Development' (OJ 2006/C46/01), which was subsequently discussed by the European Council, i.e. at the level of heads of state or government. The document reflects the EU's willingness to make a decisive contribution to the eradication of poverty in the world in general, and advancing policy coherence for development in particular. For the first time, a common vision and set of objectives, values and principles for all EU development work were provided, which centred on the achievement of the MDGs. A particular emphasis was placed on the need for coherence among external EU policies that affect developing countries. In the 'Consensus document', PCD is defined as "... ensuring that the EU takes account of the objectives of development cooperation in all policies that it implements which are likely to affect developing countries, and that these policies support development objectives" (see paragraph 9).

Last but not least, on 16 April 2006, the Council invited member states and the Commission to prepare a Work Programme 2006-07 for Policy Coherence for Development. The Work Programme is to set out steps to be taken by the Commission, the member states and the Council's Working Party on Development (CODEV). This study aims at contributing to ongoing discussions in CODEV and the informal PCD network on the PCD Work Programme and in particular to those focusing on Council procedures,[8] as well as to future discussions on PCD, such as in relation to the first PCD biennial report, due in 2007.

---

[8] This issue was mentioned in the May 2005 Council Conclusions as cited above and repeated in the April 2006 Council Conclusions that called for a review and improvement of "the Council's decision-making processes to ensure effective integration of development concerns in EU decisions in full compliance with existing competence and procedures, after preparation by Coreper", as a priority for action on PCD.

Table 1. Chronology of EU key events on PCD

Year	Key events
1993	Maastricht Treaty enters into force and establishes an explicit treaty basis for policy coherence for development
2000	Member states adopt the Millennium Development Goals (MDGs)
2003	Establishment of informal network of policy coherence for development
2005 (April)	Commission Communications on accelerating progress towards attaining the MDGs, including a Communication on PCD
2005 (May)	Council Conclusions on PCD adopted by the GAERC
2005 (December)	EU Consensus on Development adopted by European Council, Commission and European Parliament
2006 (March)	Commission staff working paper on PCD work programme 2006-07
2006 (April)	Council Conclusions on PCD Work Programme 2006-07 adopted by the GAERC

4. Analysing EU Policy-Making and PCD in 12 Policy Areas

The EC Treaty requires EU policies to be consistent (Art. 3). As with all advanced governance structures, however, EU policy-making cannot be done by one omniscient entity. In order to grasp the complexity of policy problems, to set policy objectives, to consider solutions and instruments and to ensure the democratic legitimacy of policy-making, an elaborate division of labour is necessary. In the EU we can find a complex system of governance based on the principal institutions (i.e. the Council, the Commission and the European Parliament) in which various sector-specific bodies represent different interests (e.g. Council formations, directorates general and committees). This has led to a compartmentalisation of policy-making and policy decisions and hence risks undermining policy coherence (Peterson, 2001: 302).

Table 2. Balancing interests in the EU: Key actors in the EU institutions

	Primary interest focus		
	Sector-specific	General	Development
European Commission	Sector DG	Secretariat General & other DGs	DG Development & DG AIDCO
	Portfolio Commissioner	Commission President and other Commissioners (gathering in the College of Commissioners)	Commissioners for Development and Humanitarian Aid
	Cabinet member of portfolio Commissioner	Cabinet members of Commissioners	Cabinet member responsible for development cooperation
	Sector-specific interest groups, comitology committees and advisory bodies	Other interest groups that are being consulted (e.g. consumer associations, labour unions, NGOs)	Actors being consulted focusing on development issues (e.g. development NGOs)
European Parliament	Lead Committee	Other committees, rapporteur, shadow rapporteurs, political groups when balancing interests	Development Committee
EU Council	Sectoral Council formations	GAERC European Council	GAERC
	Coreper I or II (sometimes by-passed)		Coreper II
	Specific Working Party		CODEV
	MS representative responsible for dealing with the issue at stake	Colleagues from other ministries	Colleagues from the development sector

From a legal, societal and efficiency point of view, however, it is undesirable for policies to contradict one another. Governance structures therefore generally foresee a number of administrative mechanisms intended to work towards coherence. In addition, inviting the participation of a plurality of actors should ensure that key aspects will not be completely overlooked. In general, there is a mix of actors who pursue either 'sector-specific' or 'general' interests. It is furthermore expected that ultimately interests are balanced and prioritised in the final decisions taken by democratically-chosen politicians who bear the responsibility and can be held accountable by the electorate.

Table 2 provides an overview of the key actors in each of the three major EU institutions, depending upon whether sector-specific policy, general or development interests are at stake. There are mechanisms in place to ensure that the interests of all these actors are taken into consideration in the decision-making process. At the Commission level, these include the inter-service consultation, which is intended to ensure the involvement of all relevant DGs in policy proposals, the impact assessments being made and the vote by simple majority taken in the College of Commissioners on all policy proposals (see also section 5). In the European Parliament, the most important mechanism to balance interests is the vote in plenary, as well as the reports made by committees that are not in the lead on a particular dossier. In the EU Council, as will be further elaborated upon in section 7, mechanisms are less developed, as it is argued that coordination of interests should take place 'at home', i.e. they are to be incorporated in the national position that member state representatives bring to the Council meetings.

4.1   Commission-led vs member state-led policies

For analytical purposes, one can distinguish between 'Commission-led policies' and 'member state-led policies'. The difference between the two is that the European Commission plays a more important role in the former in shaping policy and by extension ensuring coherence, whereas in the latter the EU member states in the Council and notably the EU presidency have a more prominent role in steering policies.

In general where there is an EC competence, policies are Commission-led (i.e. the pillar 1 policies). In many areas, however, the EC's competence is not exclusive, meaning that EU policies are complemented by policies at the national level or only exist to the extent that they are allowed by member states. Examples are environmental policy, where competences are shared, or research, social and employment policy, where the EC only has a complementary competence.[9] It should also be noted that external action in areas where the EU does not have an exclusive competence is usually member-state led.[10]

Many policies in the areas we have analysed for this study can be coined 'Commission-led', as they are initiated by the Commission and are otherwise strongly influenced by activities in the Commission (comitology, monitoring enforcement, etc.). This is particularly the case for the areas of trade, agriculture and fisheries where the European Community has an exclusive competence. Also in the areas of environment, climate change, transport, energy (in so far as it is linked to the internal market), information society, research, employment and social policy and migration, many policies are initiated by the Commission, although national policies also exist in these areas and external action is usually member-state led.[11]

Security policy is clearly dominated by the member states. Although the office of the High Representative for the Common Foreign and Security Policy, with its supporting policy unit, plays an increasingly important role on CFSP issues, its role is not comparable to that of a supranational entity like the European Commission. Another area that is member state-led is Justice and Home Affairs, but here some issues, including migration, have been transferred to the Community pillar and hence have become Commission-led. Generally speaking, the Community method of decision-making is used for Commission-led policies (see Figure 1), while the intergovernmental method of decision-making applies to member state-led policies (see Figure 2).

---

[9] We do not analyse the use of the open method of coordination as used in the field of research and social and employment policy. For a specific analysis of how this method contributes to PCD, please see the relevant fiches.

[10] In areas where competences are shared between the European Community and the member states, it is up to the member states to decide whether to grant the Commission the authority to represent them. Usually they do not grant this authority to the Commission and decide that the EU presidency is to represent them as well as the European Community (see Eeckhout, 2004 and Dutzler, 2002). For further details on the reach of the Commission's activities, please see the fiches and the case studies.

[11] Ibid.

Figure 1. The policy-making process in Commission-led policy areas:
The Community method of decision-making

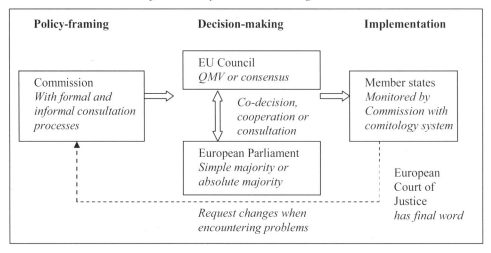

Figure 2. The policy-making process in member state-led policy areas:
The intergovernmental method of decision-making

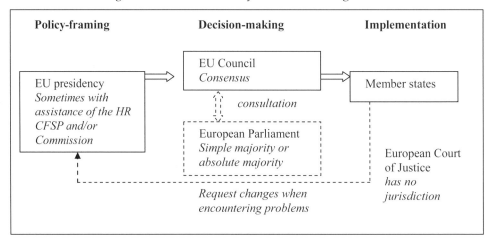

5.   Strengthening PCD in the EU Council

The input of EU member states to the Council bodies is intended to reflect a coordinated national position, thereby ensuring policy coherence. Research indicates, however, that in reality sectoral interests dominate in many of the sector-specific Council formations (e.g. Environment, Agriculture and Fisheries) and notably in the subordinate bodies where allegedly most of the decisions are actually being taken (it is estimated that 70% of the issues are solved at the WP level and 15% at the Coreper level, leaving only 15% for the Ministerial level).[12]

For instance, Hayes-Renshaw & Wallace (2006: 44) argue that in the Agriculture and Fisheries Councils, Ministers seem to have more in common with each other, in spite of national differences, than with their colleagues in national cabinets, with whom they compete for resources and priority. The common orientation appears to be even stronger at the lower levels where specialists prepare decision-making or consider implementation measures in comitology[13] committees (Beyers & Trondall, 2004, Puetter, 2004, Dehousse, 2003 and Egeberg et al., 2003). Moreover, studies have pointed to the dominance of issue networks surrounding EU decision-makers, composed of specialists and interest groups, which reinforce sectoral interests (Peterson & Bomberg, 1999, Kohler-Koch & Eising, 1999, Daugbjerg, 1999 and Richardson, 2000), sometimes to the detriment of coherence.

A number of mechanisms are in place to ensure policy coherence in the various Council formations. The principal formation is the General Affairs and External Relations Council (GAERC), which coordinates the work in other Council formations. Cross-cutting topics, especially of high political significance such as the Lisbon agenda, security or long-term climate change strategy, are often guided by the European Council. In addition, the rotating EU presidency maintains oversight of the business dealt with in the Council. All files pass through Coreper, with the aim of attaining a balance of interests, although its oversight role is undermined by its division into two entities: Coreper I and Coreper II.[14] In addition, Coreper as a whole may lack sufficient detailed knowledge to ensure PCD.

---

[12] See Hayes-Renshaw & Wallace (2006) for a comprehensive overview on the EU Council of Ministers.

[13] It is disputed whether comitology committees fall within the remit of the Commission (as it chairs them) or the Council (since the committees are installed by Council decisions and composed of member states' representatives).

[14] Coreper I consists of the deputy permanent representatives and covers most of the files related to the EU's internal market. Coreper II consists of the permanent representatives and covers the more politically sensitive issues, such as foreign policy, finance, etc. (see also Figure 3 and the organigrams in the fiches in Part II).

Figure 3. Overview of the Council bodies

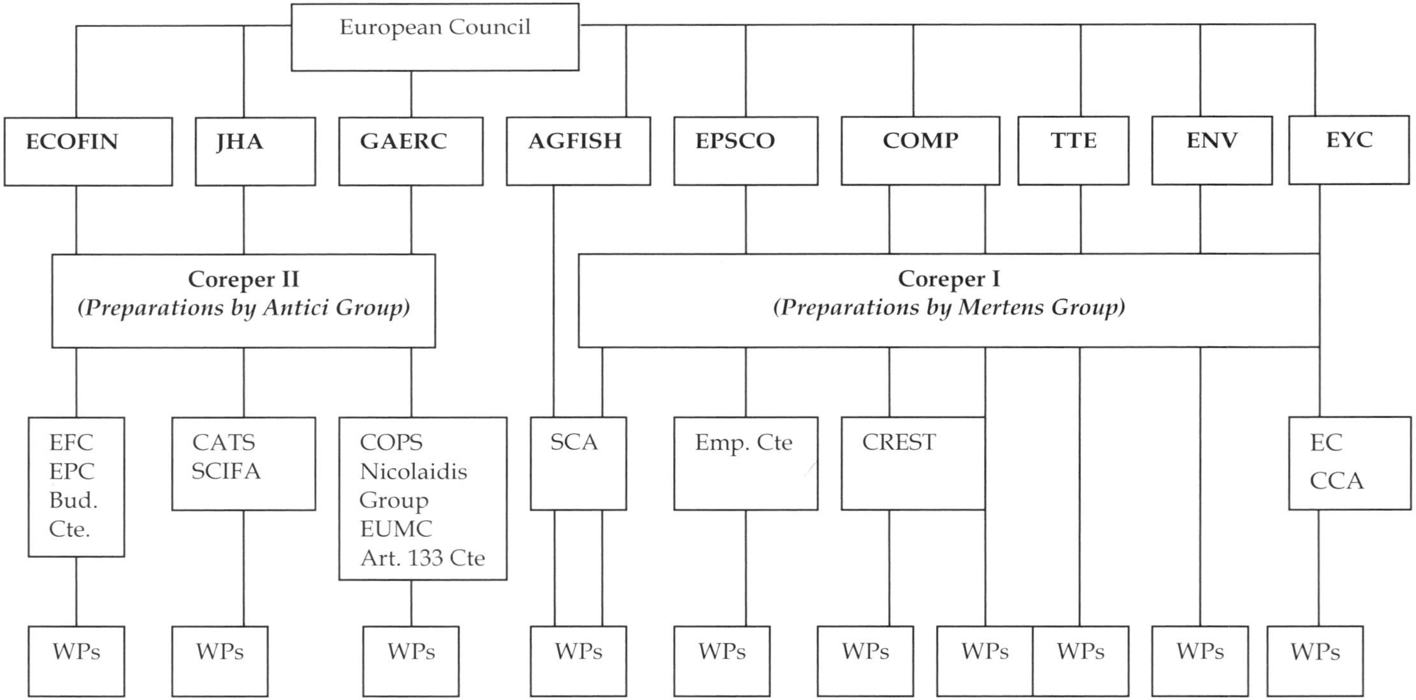

Legend (in order of appearance):

ECOFIN	Economic & Financial Affairs	Bud Cte	Economic & Financial Committee
JHA	Justice & Home Affairs	CATS	Comité Article 36 (JHA)
GEARC	General Affairs & External Relations	SCIFA	Strategic Committee on Immigration, Frontiers and Asylum
AGFISH	Agriculture & Fisheries	COPS	Comité de politique et sécurité (Political & Security Committee in English)
EPSCO	Employment, Social Policy, Health & Consumer Affairs	Art 133 Cte	Article 133 Committee (trade)
COMP	Competitiveness: Internal Market, Industry & Research	SCA	Special Committee on Agriculture
TTE	Transport, Telecommunications & Energy	Emp. Cte	Employment Committee
ENV	Environment	CREST	Committee on Scientific &Technical Research
EYC	Education, Youth & Culture	EC	Education Committee
EFC	Economic & Financial Committee	CCA	Committee on Cultural Affairs
EPC	Economic Policy Committee	WPs	Working Parties

Source: Hayes-Renshaw & Wallace (2006: 71, with modifications).

It is furthermore possible to bring together sectoral interests by organising combined Council working party (WP) meetings, but there is a risk that the meetings would become unmanageable. It is already difficult to reach agreement just among sectoral specialists. Joint meetings would add substantially to the number of people present at Council meetings and might lead to situations where two or more officials from one member state bring forward different positions. This would contradict the character of the Council as the EU institution where the interests of member state governments are to be represented. That being said, a so-called 'Friends of the Presidency Group'[1] has recently been established for the review of the Sustainable Development Strategy in which member states were asked to send delegations comprising a variety of sectoral specialists. Since the Friends of the Presidency group is seldom used and studied, it is difficult to draw conclusions on its actual and potential contribution to policy coherence.

Since the Council structure is composed of several levels (see Figure 3) we distinguish in our analysis between various layers: the European Council, the rotating EU presidency, the various Council formations existing at the ministerial level, Coreper, the senior committees, the working parties and the Council Secretariat. An analysis is also made of the European Commission, both of its internal policy-making processes and of its role in the Council, as well as of the comitology committees.

5.1 The European Council matters

In recent years, the European Council has become increasingly important in providing direction and brokering trade-offs on major issues. Although its formal and informal summits and decisions are for the most part not legally binding – its so-called 'Presidency Conclusions' have considerable political weight for EU developments.

In the various fiches, we have seen that the European Council, reinforced at times by the EU presidency, has played a significant role in promoting PCD. For example, it played an important role in ensuring a comprehensive approach to migration, climate change, energy and

---

[1] Formed at the initiative of the EU presidency, such groups aim to tackle specific policy issues that are difficult to address within existing preparatory bodies. Its membership is also determined by the presidency, hence the name.

sustainable development (see the relevant fiches and case studies). The European Council furthermore emphasised the importance it attaches to PCD by explicitly acknowledging the European Consensus on Development.

The European Council is particularly influential in setting the policy framework with regard to the CFSP, as it agrees the Common Strategies (the instruments used to pursue foreign policy aspirations). In undertaking this task, development concerns are taken into account in connection with discussions on countries with which the EU has extensive development cooperation ties, e.g. Africa (see the fiche on EU security policy).

Since PCD is a cross-cutting issue and since non-development EU policies can at times have significant impact on developing countries, it would seem a relevant topic for the European Council to discuss periodically.

5.2   The EU presidency as an important source of leadership

The EU presidency can be an important source of leadership in the EU, and member states see their turn at the helm as a chance to leave their imprint on the EU agenda. The presidency chairs and sets the agenda of the Council meetings and represents the Council vis-à-vis other EU institutions and externally. Since it oversees the work in the Council, it takes the final decision of which Council formation deals with an issue and is therefore for instance in a position to establish high-level working parties (HLWPs). Although working on the basis of the well-established norm of neutrality, presidencies have been known to steer negotiations away from their worst alternative towards their preferred outcome (Tallberg, 2004). Various recent presidencies have given the issue of PCD due attention. Finland, which holds the helm in the second half of 2006, in particular has emphasised the importance it attaches to PCD.

Setting the agenda provides the presidency with considerable power to promote PCD. In line with the 2004-06 multi-annual strategic programme for the six forthcoming presidencies, it was the Irish and Dutch Presidencies, for example, that pushed for the Action Plan to mainstream climate change into the EU's programme of development cooperation (see the case study on climate change). The Dutch (2004) and Austrian (2006) Presidencies were successful in placing the energy-development interface on the agenda by organising presidency conferences (see the fiche on energy). Another example was the Dutch Presidency Conference on "Brain Drain, the Loss of the Skills and Knowledge of Well-Trained People who Migrate to the Western World". The conference concluded that sub-Saharan Africa would be particularly vulnerable to losing its educated citizens to the Western world and argued for the establishment of a targeted cooperation programme (see fiche on EU research policy and migration case study on the crisis in human resources for health in developing countries). A reference to the conclusions of the conference was made in the Council Conclusions. The migration fiche provides another example where presidencies were crucial with regard to the importance attached to development concerns. Whereas the Spanish Presidency in 2002 focused mostly on restricting migration, the Greek Presidency in 2003 emphasised the potential role of migration as a tool to achieve development goals.

Presidencies can furthermore establish formal or informal groups to monitor specific topics or ask existing Council bodies to pay extra attention to an issue. The High-Level Working Group on Immigration and Asylum, for example, was asked by the UK Presidency to draft a set of conclusions regarding migration and external relations in general and policy coherence for development in particular (see migration fiche). These conclusions were adopted by the General Affairs and External Relations Council on 21 November 2005, with an eye to the Commission's Communication on a Policy Plan on Legal Migration.

The UK Presidency (2005) established the so-called 'Economic Partnership Agreements (EPA) Expert Group', consisting of representatives from member states, DGs Trade and Development and chaired by the European Commission. In addition, it established an informal EPA network of EU development and trade officials to facilitate informal dialogue and to closely coordinate action among the EU member states. Furthermore, the EPAs were discussed at the first meeting of EU directors-general of trade and development chaired by the Commission, and at the informal meeting of EU development ministers during the UK Presidency in 2005. The sharper focus on development that resulted from these initiatives led, for example, to the European Commission's Communication on Trade and Development Aspects of the EPA Negotiations published in November 2005, as well as in the EU-Africa strategic partnership agreed at the European Council in December 2005 (see case study on trade). Since then, member states have agreed with the Commission that they will jointly work to coordinate the bilateral and multilateral development assistance for EPAs.

With regard to the Sustainable Development Strategy, the Austrian Presidency had asked all Council formations to answer questions in preparation for the June European Council and some Council formations were asked to respond to specific questions. Moreover, it established a 'Friends of the Presidency Group' to prepare the meeting at the Council Working Party level (see below). In this group, environment and development interests have been represented among others (see the environment fiche).

Furthermore, the EU presidency exercises a key role in many international negotiations where it is the EU's main representative, usually in the context of the 'troika'.[2] For instance, the presidency is in the lead in most environmental negotiations, except for those that are clearly trade-related or of a bilateral nature, in which case the Commission takes the lead. In the negotiations, the EU presidency negotiates on behalf of the EU member states and the European Community on the basis of a mandate from Council meetings or 'EU coordination'[3] taking place at the international negotiations.

It is important to mention that it is usually the EU presidency that drafts the initial version of the negotiating mandate for the negotiations at which it is the Union's main representative. This strongly influences how the topic is framed and whether development aspects are incorporated from the start. Since this drafting is not subject for instance to an inter-service type of process, which is done by the Commission on its draft negotiating mandates, there is a risk that development aspects are not sufficiently integrated. On the other hand, as the officials in charge usually have little experience with drafting positions for international negotiations,

---

[2] Only in fields where the European Community has an exclusive competence does the Commission negotiate on behalf of the EU (e.g. in trade negotiations). In other areas, it is up to the EU member states to decide whether to grant the Commission authority to represent the EU. They often decide not to mandate this authority, thereby leaving the EU presidency the task of handling external representation. Many court cases have been fought over whether the EC has exclusive competence (Eeckhout, 2004).

[3] In the course of negotiating international agreements, it is common practice for EU representatives to sit together on a daily basis to coordinate a common position. In fact, these can be considered Council meetings on location.

they tend to seek advice from foreign ministries and notably the Council Secretariat (which is responsible for ensuring coherence of all activities of the Council, as elaborated below). In preparing the fiches and case studies, we encountered no instance where a presidency flagrantly ignored development aspects when leading EU negotiations. On the other hand, some concern was expressed by observers that insufficient attention was being paid by the Commission to development implications, but this might have to do with the issues it covers being more susceptible to development interests (e.g. trade, agriculture).

5.3 Ensuring coherence at the ministerial formations

The Council of the European Union, meaning the 9 formations in which the Ministers participate, is formally responsible for all decision-making (in many cases together with the European Parliament). Therefore the EU Council is often referred to as the 'Council of Ministers'. Which Council formation deals with a file influences to a large extent how the issue is discussed and which aspects are prioritised. Hence, the ministerial level and its structure need to be taken into account when discussing coherence and PCD.

Following successive reforms in 1999 and 2002, the number of formations has been scaled back from 21 to nine. The Council of Development Ministers, for example, was absorbed by the GAERC. In order to keep the agendas manageable, however, some Council configurations meet in sub-configurations (e.g. only transport ministers meet when transport issues are discussed in the Transport, Telecommunications and Energy Council). This contradicts the aim of the reform, which was to curb the sector-specific focus in the Council.

The GAERC configuration is particularly important for PCD because of its coordinating role. It has been argued that the GAERC has lost some of its coordinating powers in the last decade, due to the increased time it spends on EU external relations (see Hayes-Renshaw & Wallace, 2006). In carrying out research for some of the fiches, however, we have seen substantial contributions by the GAERC. For example, in the areas of climate change, energy and trade, there were Council Conclusions that explicitly addressed development cooperation. Involvement of the GAERC formation furthermore justifies involvement by CODEV since it prepares PCD files for the GAERC. In general, from a PCD perspective, it seems beneficial that the GAERC both looks at external relations and development, and coordinates Council activities.

The GAERC is also important because it is the primary body that prepares the meetings of the European Council. The preparation of European Council meetings provides opportunities for the GAERC to ensure the incorporation of the development perspective in presidency conclusions. Sustainable development and climate change strategies are two areas where the GAERC is clearly involved in a substantive way.

Another Council configuration that influences cross-cutting policies is the Economic and Financial Affairs (ECOFIN) Council. Our research found some instances where ECOFIN was marginally involved with regard to compensation measures being paid to developing countries (see in particular the case studies on sugar and the fisheries partnership agreements). A conclusion was that when financing decisions are taken at fora where development interests are poorly represented (e.g. the Agriculture and Finance Working Party), then decisions will take little account of development.

The Constitutional Treaty proposes the appointment of a Foreign Minister who would chair the GAERC, but it remains uncertain whether this treaty will ever enter into force. It is also unclear whether this official would eventually focus on further integration of development concerns in the EU's external relations.

5.4 Opportunities for member states and coalitions of member states

The fiches and case studies indicate the importance of single member states or coalitions of member states in shaping PCD at the EU level of governance. Some member states have been strong in pursuing the PCD agenda even when not holding the EU presidency. A good example is the Netherlands, which established the informal Policy Coherence for Development Network in the autumn of 2003. Another example is Poland's position paper on the effects of the European Partnership Agreements in developing countries (see case study on trade).

Some member states can wield a *de facto* veto power, at least in some policy areas, which can undermine policy coherence and PCD. For example, countries with major fishing fleets (e.g. Spain and France) seem to exert a preponderant influence over fisheries policy. In this particular case, other member states seem to have been particularly concerned with the Commission's activities with regard to the development angle of EU fisheries policy. Similarly, security policy tends to be dominated by the three big member states (Germany, France and the UK) – partly as a result of their military capacity. When they agree on a security issue, it is highly unlikely that any of the other member states will oppose their proposed action (see security fiche). In trade, notably France and Germany exercise a *de facto* veto position (see the trade fiche).

5.5 Coreper: Spider in the web?

In most policy areas, the work of the various sectoral working parties comes together in Coreper, before being channelled up to the relevant Council formations. Coreper is in a key position as it can agree 'A points', which are issues on which Coreper has reached agreement and that are therefore usually adopted by the Council without further discussion. Indeed, it can easily be argued that Coreper is the *best point in the Council system* where a broad overview of the entire range of EU business exists. This important function for the Council and the European Council's agenda offers important scope for improving PCD.

With regard to policy coherence for development, the differentiation between Coreper I and Coreper II is problematic as their division of tasks prevents coordination. Whereas Coreper I prepares a large number of special Council meetings (e.g. employment, internal market, industry, energy, etc.), the Councils that discuss politically sensitive areas – external relations and notably development issues (GAERC, ECOFIN, JHA) – fall within the competence of Coreper II. This division of labour could be considered a missed opportunity for using existing institutional settings to improve policy coherence for development or at least poses the question of whether the two Corepers coordinate well with each other.

In carrying out the research for the fiches and the case studies, we saw no evidence of Coreper emphasising the need for policy coherence, let alone policy coherence for development. Nor did we identify instances where the Mertens and the Antici Group, which coordinate the work of Coreper I and II respectively, played an explicit role in ensuring policy coherence.

5.6 Senior Council preparatory committees and working parties: Doing most of the work on their own?

To help in preparing the Council's work, Coreper can set up preparatory committees or working parties to carry out certain preparatory work or studies as defined and approved in advance by Coreper (Council Rules of Procedure, Art. 19.3.). Research indicates that there is often a considerable rivalry between those who sit in Coreper and those in working groups. Working group members, and particularly those sent from capitals, are generally unwilling to pass on files to Coreper out of fear that the limited knowledge on the part of the permanent representatives will dilute the quality of decision-making (Fouilleux et al., 2005). This is fuelled by a recurrent criticism on Permanent Representations that their diplomats 'go native' in Brussels.

A) Senior Council preparatory committees

Between the Coreper and working group structure, we find 12 senior preparatory committees for coordinating Council activities in specific fields (see Figure 3). Typically, they are composed of senior officials, normally carrying significant responsibility in their home ministry.

The senior Council preparatory committees have no formal decision-making powers, but as the natural forum for coordinating work, their influence can be considerable. If they are effective, most or all substantive points will have been resolved before the dossier comes to Coreper, before being in turn submitted to the Council, with little or no need for Coreper subsequently to reopen discussion (as illustrated in the fiche on the social dimension of globalisation, employment and decent work).

The Special Committee on Agriculture (SCA), which covers both agriculture and fisheries, has even obtained the right to directly submit 'A points' to the Agriculture and Fisheries (Agfish) Council on most of the topics under its remit. Although Coreper's involvement is still required on politically sensitive and budgetary issues, many decisions with key implications for the agricultural sector in developing countries are taken without its involvement (see the agriculture fiche and the case study on reform of the EU's sugar regime). Hence, Coreper's horizontal overview of issues in the field of agriculture is eroded.

The same holds true for the Political and Security Committee (PSC). The PSC is the main preparatory body on security issues in the Council. Formally, the PSC reports to Coreper II, but in practice, Coreper II has allowed security issues to be handled in the Council by the PSC. Coreper II becomes involved only when financial issues are at stake (see the security fiche). The PSC is even more relevant in terms of PCD, as it has even more independent power than for example the SCA. Whereas many important dossiers discussed in the SCA are passed on to the Agfish Council because no agreement could be found, most security issues are agreed upon in the PSC and do not even go on to the GAERC (see the security fiche).

Moreover, the Article 133 Committee[4] at times seems to have an independent life of its own. At international trade negotiations, it sidelines Coreper, as the negotiating mandate is adjusted in the course the negotiations without the involvement by Coreper. In comparison to other senior committees, the European Commission's role is more pronounced in the Article 133 Committee, meaning DG Trade.

B) Council Working Parties

It is estimated that around 250 working parties are in place to prepare the work of the Council (Hayes-Renshaw & Wallace, 2006). Some working groups are permanent, while others are ad hoc and disappear after tackling a specific question. Their relative autonomy – illustrated by the estimation that they solve some 70% of all Council work without further discussion at Coreper or the ministerial level – jeopardises coherent coordination among the policy areas (Hayes-Renshaw & Wallace, 2006). The frequency of meetings varies from one working group to another. Some meet only once or twice a month, e.g. the climate change formation of the WP International Environment Issues (IEI), whereas others meet up to four times a month, e.g. the environment and information society working groups.

There is by no means a standing operating procedure for the interaction between CODEV and the other working groups covering non-development policy areas. There is little evidence of contact, for example, between CODEV and the Working Party on Sugar and Iso-glucose. In the sugar case study, the former focused on the accompanying measures, and the latter on the nature of the EU's internal reform, two strongly related issues, but little coordination took place between them. CODEV is also not an integral participant in core trade policy debates (see the trade fiche). Although CODEV and the ACP WP attended the meetings on the EPAs (Economic Partnership Agreements) of the Article 133 Committee in May

---

[4] Named after the article in the EC Treaty covering trade policy, the Article 133 Committee is a special advisory body of the Council. See the fiche on trade policy I Part II for more discussion.

2005, they only played a limited role (see case study on the EPAs). It is also very rare for officials from development agencies to attend meetings of COARM (Council Working Group on Conventional Arms Experts), and the Code of Conduct on Arms Exports has reportedly not been discussed within CODEV (see the security case study).

On the other hand, CODEV was officially in the lead on the Climate Change Action Plan as it was the expert group the GAERC had envisaged (in its December 2003 Council Conclusions) to further discuss this document (see case study). The International Environmental Issues WP and particularly its subordinate Developing Countries expert group, given their expertise, were asked by CODEV to take care of most of the preparatory discussions on the Action Plan. This feature of the process, i.e. involving working parties from development and non-development streams, is particularly noteworthy and provides a significant contrast to, for instance, the case study on fisheries.

In energy, too, CODEV has been involved with regard to the Council Conclusions on 'integrating energy interventions into development cooperation' that were adopted by the GAERC on 10 April 2006 (see the fiche on energy).

The *'Friends of the Presidency' group* has largely been dormant, but it can be brought to life whenever the presidency needs help with a specific issue. The group, whose membership is agreed upon by the EU presidency, was started during the Portuguese Presidency in the spring of 2000, in the context of food safety. In 2004, the Dutch Presidency established a Friends of the Presidency group on the question of the start of accession negotiations with Turkey. It appointed a number of special representatives ('Friends of the Dutch presidency') to convince certain member states to reach agreement (Hayes-Renshaw & Wallace, 2006).

Recently the Austrian presidency established a 'Friends of the Presidency' group to prepare the June 2006 European Council discussion on the EU's renewed 'Sustainable Development Strategy' (see the environment fiche). It was particularly important that the group represented a broad set of interests, including environmental and development concerns, among many others. Its character has furthermore been quite different from for instance the Friends of the Presidency group the Dutch had established, in that all member states were participating and in a position to identify their delegates.

5.7   Council Secretariat: The neutral assistant?

The secretariat underpins the entire Council hierarchy. Its tasks include being a negotiations 'manager', a political counsellor to the presidency, a 'good offices' mediator and a political secretariat for the Secretary-General/High Representative, as well as assuming an executive role in planning and organising military and civilian crisis-management operations. According to the Council's Rules of Procedure (Art. 23.3), the Secretariat is responsible for "organising, coordinating and *ensuring coherence of the Council's work*" (emphasis added).

A particular role of the Council Secretariat is to provide support to the EU presidency in conducting the rotating term. It tracks the preferences and negotiating positions of all member states, provides information about EU decision-making procedures and the formal instruments available to the presidency, and is a source of expertise on the content of dossiers under negotiation (Tallberg, 2004). The importance of the Council Secretariat for each presidency varies significantly, however, depending on the presidency itself. While some actively seek such suggestions, other presidencies prefer to manage the agenda with less assistance from the Secretariat.

The Council Secretariat is expected to act in a politically neutral way in order to gain the confidence of the EU member states. It is therefore particularly unusual for Council Secretariat staff to emphasise a specific viewpoint, such as arguing for a more explicit integration of development concerns into a policy. Nevertheless, the Council Secretariat can play a role for example by ensuring that the Council Conclusions on PCD, are taken into account in relevant decisions.

In the field of the CFSP, the Council Secretariat has a special role as its Secretary-General is the High Representative for the CFSP. While major policy initiatives from the Secretariat meet with criticism, the Secretariat has become increasingly influential through a series of smaller more modest initiatives (see the security fiche). This is reflected in the considerable decline in the number of proposals submitted by the member states, as they prefer to influence the eventual decision through informal contacts with the Council Secretariat (Westlake & Galloway, 2004: 341). Nevertheless, the Council Secretariat is far from being a supranational entity for CFSP in the way that the European Commission is in other areas, as it has limited capacity, resources and competences. This reduces the scope for integrating PCD in the field of security.

5.8   A brief analysis of PCD in the European Commission

The Commission exerts a strong influence on EU policies and it is therefore important that development concerns are taken into account in its policy activities, for example when drafting policy proposals, setting technical standards or monitoring implementation. As the guardian of the treaties, the Commission is also supposed to take due account of policy coherence, both with regard to its internal policy-making processes as well as with regard to its position in the EU Council. Inside the Commission the prime responsibility for PCD resides with DG Development, which drew attention to the issue in particular by drafting the Commission's 2005 Communication on Policy Coherence for Development – Accelerating progress towards attaining the Millennium Development Goals.

The extent to which the Commission incorporates development concerns in its policy formulations has varied over the years. For example, the implications for third world countries of EU agricultural, trade and fisheries policies have tended in the past to be neglected (see the relevant fiches), but this is no surprise, as these were not political priorities at the time they were drafted. Changes have occurred, however, as a result of the increasing evidence of EU policies impacting on developing countries, a deeper understanding of the impact of the EU on world markets, the ensuing pressures from civil society and increased demands by developing countries in international negotiations. These factors have increased the awareness among EU policy-makers and the officials of the European Commission.

The implications for development of other EU policies such as information society, transport, energy (for the internal market), research and the social dimension of globalisation, employment and decent work, have been less considered. Although one should acknowledge that the Commission's draft proposals in these fields may appear on the surface to have a marginal effect on reaching the MDGs,[5] they have been identified as

---

[5] Since we did not 'measure' the impact of policies in terms of their contribution to development, we cannot draw a firm conclusion here, but several of the experts whom we interviewed indicated that they did not really see a problem in the relationship between the policy area and reaching development objectives.

relevant policy areas in the Council Conclusions on PCD. The fiches also show that there are interfaces with development objectives.[6]

Below we briefly outline some of the factors that have been decisive for PCD in the European Commission.[7]

Choice of lead DG when drafting policy proposals. An important – although not surprising – finding in the fiches is that it matters whether a non-development DG or DG Development is in the lead for a development-relevant policy proposal.[8] In the circumstance where the non-development DG was in the lead, coordination with DG Development has often been insufficient, including with regard to the impact assessments and during the inter-service consultation. Examples where DG Development was not in the lead are trade (DG Trade on the EPAs), fisheries (DG Fisheries on FPAs), migration (DG Justice, Freedom and Security on a Communication covering the relationship between migration and development) and research (DG research still working on the INCO Communication whereas FP 7 is already on the table). The reform of the EU's sugar regime is a case where DGs settled for a division of labour: DG Agriculture has been in the lead with regard to the proposal to lower subsidies for EU producers and DG Development has been in the lead with regard to the compensation measures for countries currently profiting from preferential access to the EU's sugar market. The case study illustrates that insufficient communication and coordination between the two DGs have been detrimental to PCD. In other areas, where DG Development has been in the lead under the theme of 'development first', e.g. on the Communication on Climate Change in the Context of Development Cooperation and the Communication on the EU Energy Initiative, development implications have been better integrated (see the climate change and energy fiches).

The choice of lead DG is furthermore important as it implicitly guides the assignment of which Council formation and Working Party will

---

[6] For example, in the field of research, scant attention has been given to problems of brain drain and research capacity in the Commission's proposal for the 7th Framework Programme for Research (FP 7), particularly in sub-Saharan Africa (see the fiche on research as well as the case study on migration).

[7] Since the fiches and case studies focused mainly on the Council, only tentative findings can be drawn from the analysis.

[8] In some cases, the lead of either the sector DG or DG Development could be justified.

subsequently deal with the policy proposal, although formally this decision is in the hands of the presidency. We have found only one example – migration – where a file was assigned to CODEV and the GAERC, while not being prepared by DG Development. In all other cases, files were assigned to the sector-specific Council formations and Working Party.

As could be expected, in the circumstances where DG Development was in the lead, as shown by the climate change case study, more attention was given to the development perspective from the start. However, having DG Development in the lead might not be acceptable on all files with a development aspect and therefore one could also envisage having officials in other DGs monitor whether development implications are taken into account. This is already done to ensure that economic and environmental implications are taken into account in Commission activities and proposals. Moreover, in most DGs, there are already officials responsible for developing country issues (e.g. in DG Agriculture) or international relations, whose remit is to defend development concerns. Nevertheless, as the fiches have shown, their impact is limited, due possibly to their not having sufficient authority or numbers within their DG or simply not being sufficiently aggressive.

Early consultation with member states and other stakeholders. The fiches demonstrate that various DGs are actively engaged in consultation rounds with civil society, business as well as with member states when drafting policy initiatives. In some cases, the Commission has also engaged in consultations with developing countries. However, the fiches show little evidence that legitimate – even if debatable – concerns by developing countries or development interest groups, including NGOs, expressed in consultation rounds (e.g. sugar reform or fisheries agreements), have been sufficiently taken into account by the lead DG in charge. A notable exception has been migration (see case study on the brain drain in the health sector), which illustrates the successful attempt by a member state, in this case the UK, to integrate development concerns into a policy proposal by the Commission. Council Working Parties and individual representatives from member states seem to plead actively with the Commission to take certain issues into account. This confirms other studies (e.g. Peterson, 2001) that emphasise that the Commission's power of initiative is in reality diluted by member states, when they attempt to influence the EU agenda.

A particular area for initiative by member states or interest groups – through formal or informal processes – could be advocacy for new Commission proposals, pushing the integration of development and non-development policies further. Examples we identified were research projects in least-developed countries similar to the European and Developing Country Trials Partnership (EDCTP) project (see fiche on research policy) or Communications covering the little-explored relationship between development and transport, information society or the social dimension of globalisation, employment and decent work. The inclusion of these areas in the Council Conclusions on PCD has been a first step to increase awareness. Further awareness and understanding of the relationship between non-development policies and development objectives could be expected by either DG Development prioritising the analysis of development aspects of non-development policies, or alternatively, other DGs appointing (additional) development liaison officers.

Inter-service consultation on policy proposals. Policy proposals drafted by a DG are subject to consultation with other DGs. The process is described in the Commission's rules of procedure.[9] The procedure varies depending on the nature, scope and urgency of the proposal and is relatively flexible to work with. In practice, standing formal and informal consultation groups are in place in many areas to ensure coordination between the Commission's services. For example, in the EPA case study, a more or less fixed group was identified that looked after the EPA negotiations (see the trade case study). For development-related topics, usually the officials covering international issues participate in inter-service consultation meetings.

It is relevant to mention here that the Legal Service has a special position as it checks consistency with other legislation and with the treaties, and is also always present in the meetings of the College of Commissioners to explain its legal opinion on a proposal. In some cases, it has not shied away from blocking proposals in the inter-service consultation.

Several of the fiches and notably the case studies (see the examples above) suggest that DG Development has played a limited role during the inter-service consultation on issues affecting developing countries. It could be the case that it was not invited, but the impression was that DG

---

[9] OJ L 308/26 of 8 December 2000.

Development did not actively pursue its mandate. This is a missed opportunity as DG Development's active involvement in inter-service consultations is crucial for PCD.

It could, for example, (threaten to) block a policy proposal by suspending the procedure or by giving a negative opinion when it considers that the development aspects have been ignored. Such a negative opinion could still be ignored by the College of Commissioners and generally, threatening to block a proposal is considered rather exceptional. Nevertheless, a more assertive DG Development in cases where development interests are at stake would give a strong signal that the development aspects of non-development policies are to be taken seriously. A more assertive DG Development would almost certainly raise awareness on PCD as a whole, impacting far beyond the political level of the Commission.

In addition, it would be important to make development aspects and possible impacts on developing countries more explicit in Commission proposals, and to do so in a way that is understandable to non-specialists as well (particularly with regard to technical files, such as those on food standards, fishery stocks, etc.). In order to achieve this, sufficient capacity in DG Development to monitor and participate in inter-service consultations (i.e. by staff with sufficient skills to master the technical files) would be needed. A potential ally for a more critical position in the inter-service consultation would be the Legal Service, which is bound to ensure that EU actions adhere to EU laws and decisions.

For urgent issues, a 'fast track' inter-service procedure is sometimes used, where consultation is done at the level of Commissioners and their cabinets (by-passing the inter-service consultation). On these, the lead DG has a strong influence, as it decides which DGs to consult and the timing of the inter-service consultation. However, neglecting an associated DG or forgetting to invite a DG can cause the procedure to encounter major problems and de facto can block the preparation of the proposal. One should also note that this procedure applies only to a minority of proposals and from a PCD perspective, should be avoided as much as possible.

Integrated impact assessments of policy proposals. When considering major new policy initiatives, the Commission is mandated to obtain an *ex post* evaluation of the existing policy. Simultaneously and in the run-up to the inter-service consultation, the lead DG undertakes an *ex ante* impact assessment, to which other DGs can provide input. In reality, the evaluation of the existing situation is often still going on while the new proposal has already been drafted, thereby undermining the impact assessment tool.

Recent analyses of the impact assessment process indicate that the external dimension of proposals is insufficiently taken into account, if at all (Renda, 2006; Opoku & Jordan, 2004). For example, the sustainable development aspect of proposals is assessed mainly on the basis of environmental criteria and less so on the implications for the economic development of developing countries. Several fiches and case studies revealed a perception that DG Development is not actively engaged in the impact assessment process. Among the potential reasons were that impact assessments were not considered a priority or were seen as too difficult to follow (i.e. too technical), or that DG Development suffers from a lack of resources.

Such a lack of resources may partly explain why, according to Renda (2006), DG Development also underperforms when it comes to making extended impact assessments on its own proposals. In any event, several activities of the Commission fall outside the scope of the impact assessment process. For example, the trade fiche points out that the negotiating directives for trade negotiations are only subject to impact assessment after they have been tabled, thereby limiting the role of impact assessments in changing a proposal. The fisheries fiche suggests that impact assessments, which in theory should analyse alternative policy options to select the most suitable one, in reality are drafted to support the Commission's preferred course of action. This characteristic of the impact assessment, justifying preferred options, was also highlighted by Renda (2006) as one of the main constraints to better policy-making.

Although not strictly belonging to the Commission's impact assessment procedure, the fisheries case study and fiche also highlight the importance of having proper policy impact analyses. Since assessments on available fish stocks were often of poor quality, it became difficult to determine the level of financial compensation offered to the developing countries whose fish stocks were depleted by fishing fleets of EU member states.

Approval of Policy Proposals in the College of Commissioners. Commission proposals have to be approved by a simple majority in the College of Commissioners, which includes the Commissioner responsible for Development. In carrying out their assessments of proposals, Commissioners draw heavily on their cabinets. Although the role of cabinets has not been examined in the fiches, it is evident from a PCD perspective that it would be beneficial if cabinet members responsible for development paid attention to non-development policies with indirect implications for developing countries. This task is certainly a challenge given the limited size of the cabinets, but it could be facilitated if DG Development monitored and assessed policy proposals in greater detail. Also, the Commissioner for Development and the cabinet should agitate for sufficient attention to the development perspective in relevant proposals.

The Commission in the EU Council. Once a proposal has reached the Council, the Commission is involved in the negotiations and is in charge of introducing amendments. In that way, the Commission can ensure that the draft laws are in line with the EU policy stance on development. The fiches and case studies, however, do not provide examples where Commission officials participating in Council bodies have emphasised the importance of development concerns when member states argued for amendments diluting the development focus (e.g. the increased income support level for EU sugar producers or the stance on agricultural subsidies in the WTO negotiations). On the contrary, we have seen several instances where individual member states have pressed the Commission to take account of development concerns (see also the previous section on the Council).

The role of comitology and expert groups chaired by the Commission in framing and monitoring policies. In areas such as agriculture, fisheries, environment, transport, information society and the social dimension of globalisation, employment and decent work, the fiches illustrate the influential role of technical committees and expert groups chaired by the Commission in shaping the implications of EU directives and regulations. Often these groups are the first places where problems with implementation of current directives arise and they can therefore be an important informal catalyst for policy change. The problem with the committees is their primary focus on the technical issue without being able to place it in a broader policy context, let alone to examine the implications for developing countries. Hence it can happen that a technical committee decides on stricter sanitary and phytosanitary standards (e.g. traceability obligations) for the EU's internal market (and presses them at the level of the WTO), without realising the implications for producers in developing countries already having difficulties with fulfilling existing standards for exports to the EU.

6. Drivers for Change

We have seen in the previous sections that numerous opportunities for enhancing PCD exist both in the Council and the Commission. The analysis and findings contained in the fiches and the case studies also demonstrate, however, that these opportunities are not always used and that dedicated structures or actors to monitor PCD still need to be set up or assigned.

This section discusses drivers for change that could be mobilised to ensure implementation of these or other recommendations, ideas and insights for strengthening the PCD focus in EU policy-making. We identify the following categories of drivers derived from DFID (2003): i) political will, commitment and leadership; ii) strategies; iii) institutional capacity; iv) awareness and institutional culture and v) accountability.

6.1 Political will, commitment, leadership

Leadership provides the overall direction and has the capacity to manage change. The analysis reveals that leadership on PCD can be and has been undertaken at various levels and by different actors. It can only be successfully exercised when backed by overall political will and commitment at the highest political level.

To strengthen the importance attached to PCD in EU policy-making processes, support by the *European Council* is crucial, as it represents the highest political level. Thus far, we have seen positive contributions by the European Council on the issue of PCD, which could be strengthened, for instance by discussing PCD periodically and keeping PCD in mind in discussions on the areas mentioned in the Council Conclusions on PCD. A second key actor is the *presidency*, which can (and has) initiate(d) numerous formal and informal initiatives to strengthen PCD. A third actor is the *GAERC*. By combining its insights on external relations and development with its function of coordinating the business of other Council formations, it can contribute much to increasing the awareness of development concerns. A fourth actor is the *European Commission and in particular DG Development*. The Commission can prioritise development concerns in relevant proposals and can initiate new policy activities on the relationship between the 12 areas and development objectives.

6.2 Strategies

A strategy calls for clarity of vision. It generally consists of a formal mission statement and a set of goals, as well as a plan of action for achieving the necessary changes to meet those goals.

With regard to PCD, we see various well-defined strategies that outline the problem and call for action (most of them are relatively recent). They include the MDG focus on policy coherence, the priority attached to PCD in the European Consensus on Development, the Council Conclusions on PCD and the Work Programme that is now under discussion. The quality of the latter initiative will be crucial as it will set out the areas for further action on PCD.

In non-development policy areas, we have found different degrees to which the relationship with development has been examined. In many instances, this relationship has not been framed properly and remains sketchy and ad hoc in nature.[10] A certain level of understanding, however, is essential for being able to identify strategies to improve PCD. Moreover, having a clear strategy in place is crucial in order to establish leadership, or to provide sufficient institutional capacity and resources. Even in areas where the relationship with development cooperation is better defined,[11] there is still not always a comprehensive strategy in place. There is a need to increase the understanding of the link between development cooperation objectives and the policy areas covered in the Council Conclusions on PCD by the European Commission, the various Council bodies, the EU presidency and if appropriate the Council Secretariat. This could be achieved in several ways, for example, by organising training programmes for EU civil servants, or Presidency- or Commission-sponsored workshops or by issuing new Commission Communications.

6.3 Institutional capacity

Institutional capacity and resources define clear lines of accountability/responsibility, i.e. the number of management levels in an

---

[10] Examples include transport, information society, research and social and employment policy.

[11] Examples include trade, agriculture, fisheries, security and migration.

organisation, coordination mechanisms, key decision-making, communication and control relationships, but also the number of officials involved. The issue includes having sufficient skills and knowledge to deal with the content of the policy.

The number of staff members is crucial as well as their authority within their organisation and the magnitude of resources placed at their disposal. We have seen several instances where capacity seemed insufficient, e.g. lack of awareness, late involvement of development specialists, inadequate handling of Commission inter-service consultation or impact assessments. There is also a question whether the GAERC Council devotes enough time and resources to investigate the link between development cooperation objectives and non-development policies. Discussions on PCD automatically involve CODEV. The informal network on PCD could help by providing more input into CODEV, but questions remain as to its status and role in driving change in politically sensitive areas.

It requires considerable expertise to cover the relationship between development and (the 12) other policy areas. Significant technical knowledge is required in order to identify the development component (e.g. the impacts of technical agricultural decisions on developing country producers), let alone to ensure PCD. Having specialists with the right skills is therefore essential when attempting to improve the quality of a proposal or an impact assessment. This requires devoting more effort to improving the skills of officials at all levels in the Commission, member states (including the permanent representation staff) and in the Council Secretariat. An analogous programme was recently instituted by the European Commission as part of its administrative reform, aimed at upgrading the skills of officials at all levels. The system could incorporate training for officials on the development implications of EU actions. The issues of training and mutual learning could be further investigated in studies focusing on improving coordination on PCD at the member state level.

Generally speaking, civil service systems in which officials rotate regularly between various DGs and between different ministries are more likely to produce better policy coherence. Civil servants who have spent time in a variety of DGs can be expected to have a better perception of the perspectives of other policy fields. One could also think about exchange programmes for officials (e.g. the twinning programmes) so that officials from different member states could learn from each others' knowledge and experiences.

6.4 Awareness and organisational culture

Organisational culture encompasses the covert and overt rules, values, customs and principles that guide the behaviour of the members of an organisation. The introduction of consultative/participatory processes in the organisation may support or hinder reform by changing this culture.

Formal and informal consultation procedures shape EU policy-making within the Council framework. Expert groups or informal networks, for example, are created to set the agenda, prepare initiatives and build consensus and support. Setting up an expert group can be used as a means to invite relevant interests early in the policy-making process to conduct a kind of (pre-) negotiation, and hence could be an efficient tool to integrate development concerns into policy-making at an early stage.

A recurring theme in the fiches and case studies is that it is not considered appropriate to follow too closely the business of other Council formations or working parties. For policy coherence, including PCD, however, such sensitivities are not very constructive. Another issue was that development specialists tend to devote most of their attention to aid-related topics, such as compensation measures. This at times seems to have distracted attention from the actual policies and proposed policy changes that invoke the need for these compensation measures.

Transparency and access of interest groups and developing country representatives to documents and policy-makers might also increase the awareness of development aspects in the policy-making process. EU actions and policies are still to a large extent non-transparent, if only because the governance structure is relatively sophisticated and complex. Transparency is difficult to decree by regulation, however, and therefore depends heavily on political leadership.

6.5 Accountability

Development issues do not directly affect the lives of EU citizens, but many are concerned about the poor in this world, as indicated by the results of several Eurobarometer surveys and membership enrolment in development NGOs. The EU itself also tends to emphasise the importance of normative issues in international affairs, including sustainable development, poverty reduction and human rights (Manners, 2002; Emerson, 2005).

In practice, however, it appears rather difficult to ensure that the EU does what it promises and to ensure, for example, that the viewpoints of developing countries are taken into account in internal EU decisions with external implications. In general the role of national parliaments as political watchdogs, often catalysed by critical reports in the media, is important.

It is often difficult, however, for parliamentarians to follow what their ministers do in Brussels, although in recent years some measures have been made to improve the transparency of the Council's activities (Hayes-Renshaw & Wallace, 2006). There are also significant differences with regard to the extent to which parliaments can control their ministers (Lord, 2005). It might be interesting to investigate these differences in further detail in the context of ensuring PCD at the member state level.

The European Parliament wields considerable influence on policies that are decided by co-decision. Indeed in the relevant areas, the Presidency and Council Secretariat devote much of their time in consultation with the EP on files that are handled under the rules of co-decision (Hayes-Renshaw & Wallace, 2006). Nevertheless, there are still issues with relevance for PCD (e.g. agriculture, external action) where co-decision does not apply. Although the EP can still exert some influence in these fields through its resolutions, this does not compensate for the lack of co-decision powers. Although granting more power to parliaments is no guarantee for increased PCD, their involvement would allow political choices to be made in a more transparent and accountable way.

In order to ensure that development concerns remain on the radar screen of parliamentarians, it is important to keep them well-informed. Information could be provided directly by development specialists from the Commission, the member states, independent experts, NGOs and the media. Their argumentation would be strengthened when based on independent and authoritative reports and evaluations. For instance, the Work Programme on PCD (and its successors) could become the subject of an external evaluation.

Implementation and evaluation are keys to accountability. We know that member states do not always fully implement policies decided upon in the EU into national legislation or do not fully enforce them. When implementing EU policies, the PCD aspects should not be neglected by the EU member states (e.g. by failing to accurately check the quantity of fish caught by their fishermen in foreign waters). Also PCD actions decided upon in the Work Programme might be an issue to follow closely in the future. Implementation of relevant EU legislation is a particular issue that would deserve attention when analysing PCD at the national level.

With regard to accountability vis-à-vis the individual citizens of developing countries, it is difficult to make improvements as they by definition are excluded from the democratic decision-making processes in the EU. Nevertheless, there is longstanding tradition of consultation with the ACP (African, Caribbean and Pacific) countries, notably through a Joint Council of Ministers, a Committee of Ambassadors and a Joint Parliamentary Assembly. The ACP also maintains a secretariat in Brussels to service the relationship on a day-to-day basis. The ACP countries are furthermore involved in the administration of the European Development Fund (EDF). Such consultation efforts are important since they stimulate coherence with national development priorities, improve the quality of argumentation used by development specialists and could increase the support for and feasibility of implementing measures that are in the EU's interest (e.g. the establishment of higher food safety or environmental standards).

7. Conclusions: A Strategy for Strengthening PCD in the Council

The main objective of this study has been to examine whether policy-making processes in the EU Council on non-development policies sufficiently allow for 'development-related' inputs in order to ensure policy coherence with EU development objectives, i.e. to ensure at a minimum that domestic EU policies do not undermine development objectives. In addition, the study has looked at the policy-making processes in the European Commission in its role of initiating and defending most of the policies being discussed in the Council.

It is important to keep in mind that the powers of the Commission and the Council vary depending upon the policy area, as a result of varying Community competencies and decision-making procedures. Generally speaking, achieving coherence in the Commission is similar to achieving coherence in a nation state (intra-governmental coherence), whereas achieving coherence in the Council requires bringing in line the efforts of several countries (inter-governmental coherence). This implies *inter alia* that coherence in the Council depends to a large extent on the coordination of national inputs in the decision-making system. Nevertheless, there are also many ways to strengthen policy coherence for development at the Council level.

This study has reviewed the multiple layers of the EU Council structure in a broad and non-legal sense, including the European Council, the rotating EU presidency, the ministerial formations, Coreper, the senior committees, the working parties and the Council Secretariat. We also analysed, to a lesser extent, the Commission and its comitology committees.

By and large, *the European Council*, reinforced at times by the EU presidency, has played a significant role in promoting PCD. Of particular benefit to PCD is the fact that in the preparation of summits, all Council formations through the GAERC and their own conclusions can provide input to the groundwork and the subsequent presidency conclusions. However, only a minority of issues are covered by the European Council. Since PCD is a cross-cutting issue in the external relations of the EU, the European Council could consider discussing it as a full agenda item more often in the future, for instance once every year or every other year.

The presidency chairs and sets the agenda of the Council meetings, and represents the Council vis-à-vis other EU institutions and externally. In particular, the functions of setting the agenda gives the presidency considerable power to promote PCD. Presidencies can also establish formal or informal groups to monitor specific topics or ask existing Council bodies to pay extra attention to an issue. It is important for presidencies to pay sufficient attention to PCD in international negotiations.

In addition, the study has identified the importance of efforts by *single member states* or coalitions of member states to ensure policy coherence for development at the EU level. It is important for member states to continue to pursue the PCD agenda when they are not in the presidency, for instance by emphasising development implications in relevant decisions, publishing position papers, commissioning independent studies or organising conferences or workshops.

GAERC's performance on PCD has been uneven, which calls for exploring ways to ensure GAERC's involvement in PCD in a more systematic way. The more intensively the GAERC deals with policy coherence for development, the more *CODEV* as its preparatory body on these matters, would be able to concentrate on PCD matters. In a more general sense, increased GAERC attention to both external relations and development is warranted, when it is coordinating Council activities. Development ministers could provide more weight to PCD by participating in more meetings of the GAERC, notably when trade or another external issue with implications for developing countries is discussed.

Coreper is very important for PCD: as for most policy files, the work of the various sectoral working parties comes together in Coreper, before being channelled up to the relevant Council formations. Coreper is in a key position as it not only prepares the decisions for the ministers but it also can reach agreement itself by issuing 'A points'. In order to achieve greater policy coherence for development, more attention needs to be paid to the issue and more information needs to be received on development aspects of files and disseminated, particularly to Coreper I as it normally does not follow development issues. In this respect, it is of crucial importance that Coreper receives adequate information by the Council preparatory bodies, i.e. the Senior Committees and Working Parties. Among the six structural reforms we propose below, two are aimed (see nos. 2 and 3) at increasing the information Coreper receives from the preparatory bodies. Furthermore, it is important that Coreper does not hesitate to reopen files when there are indications that development concerns have not been sufficiently taken into account.

The study has identified five crucial areas affecting policy coherence in the *European Commission*.

1. *Choice of the lead DG in charge of drafting policy proposals.* In the circumstances when non-development DGs have been in the lead, coordination with DG Development has generally been poor.

2. *The importance of early consultation with member states and with stakeholders.* The study demonstrates that the various DGs are actively engaged in consultation with civil society, business as well as with member states when drafting policy initiatives and in some cases with representatives of developing countries. We found little evidence that concerns expressed by the latter or development NGOs have been sufficiently taken into account by the lead DG in charge. Improvements are needed to ensure that the views of all legitimate stakeholders are taken into consideration.

3. *Inter-service consultation and integrated impact assessments on policy proposals.* In theory, DG Development is consulted on any policy proposal that might have implications for developing countries and is in a position to provide input to the impact assessment of these

proposals. This study has found that DG Development underperforms in this area and recommends that DG Development should strengthen its efforts to ensure that the development aspect and possible impacts on developing countries become more explicit in Commission proposals, and that these impacts are expressed in terms that are understandable to non-specialists as well.

4. *Approval of policy proposals in the College of Commissioners.* Commission proposals have to be approved by a simple majority in the College of Commissioners, which includes the commissioner responsible for development. The commissioner for development therefore needs to be a strong advocate for PCD. As commissioners rely heavily on their cabinets, it would be beneficial for cabinet members responsible for development to pay close attention to non-aid policies that have indirect implications for developing countries. This could be facilitated by DG Development monitoring and assessing policy proposals in greater detail.

5. *The Commission in the EU Council.* Once a policy proposal is in the Council, the Commission is involved in the negotiations, notably by introducing amendments. Therefore the Commission has a special responsibility to ensure that its policy initiatives stay in line with the EU policy stance on development, but this has rarely happened. Accordingly, there is a need for the Commission to more actively promote PCD during Council negotiations.

7.1 Six proposals for structural reform

1. Strengthen accountability in the Council of Ministers

A first proposal is to strengthen the accountability of what ministers do in the Council formations, including their stance on PCD and how EU PCD objectives are incorporated. Accountability in the EU is strengthened by the involvement of the European Parliament and transparency requirements. While the European Parliament plays a strong role under co-decision, many files that are important for PCD (agriculture and external relations) are exempted from this procedure. Hence, the European Parliament's leverage is limited. Greater transparency and media involvement would also be beneficial for PCD. Although changes in these areas are subject to the overall discussion on institutional reform and therefore cannot be expected to be influenced in a significant way by PCD concerns, PCD is an important example illustrating the need for greater accountability. The accountability of ministers on PCD could be strengthened further by asking Council formations to periodically and publicly report to the GAERC on development implications of decisions taken, for instance linked to discussions in the GAERC on the PCD Work Programme. Independent studies could also be carried out to monitor the 'PCD-degree' of decisions taken in the areas mentioned in the PCD Council Conclusions.

2. Create and strengthen PCD expert groups

Although it is important for development concerns to be taken into account in the Council's preparatory bodies, the highly segmented character of the senior committee and working party level strengthens the sector-specific focus. In general, the higher the seniority of the participants of these bodies and the closer they are to their national ministries, the more sectoral interests prevail – to the detriment of PCD. Groups could be asked to make development aspects more explicit before a file goes to Coreper or to involve Coreper II if they find it necessary. Such a system would be hard to enforce, however. An alternative arrangement would be to allow CODEV to supplement the work of other working parties when it comes to development issues. The drawback to such a solution is that it would elevate CODEV into a 'super working party', which could arouse the suspicion of other working parties and interests, aside from the question of whether such a move would be politically acceptable. Therefore this study proposes the strengthening of existing expert groups and the creation of separate new ones focusing on the link between a policy area and development. Such expert groups would always need to be involved in policy files containing provisions with implications for developing countries. The expert group's role would be to advise the sector-specific working party and CODEV or to answer questions from them, for example as the expert group on trade and development does today. CODEV could subsequently report to Coreper II or the GAERC when it has the impression that the expert group is insufficiently involved or that its work is not taken into account in the decisions made in the relevant working party. This would also improve the accountability of the work of the working parties with regard to PCD.

In practical terms, one could envisage 12 expert groups operating alongside the areas covered in the Council conclusions. They already exist for trade (the trade and development expert group, the trade, agriculture, and development group and the EPA group) and climate change (the developing countries expert group). For some areas, the groups could be combined, for instance alongside the Council formations. The groups could be explicitly called PCD expert groups to give prominence to their PCD function. The role of the informal PCD network should be to identify common experiences in the work of the expert groups and to bring overarching PCD issues to the attention of CODEV.

3. Appoint PCD observers in senior preparatory committees

Our study has found that PCD receives minimal attention in the senior preparatory committees. This neglect, in part, is due to the fact that some of these committees (e.g. the Special Committee on Agriculture – SCA) are not integrated into the Coreper line of reporting and also because the participants are of comparable seniority to those of Coreper and tend to be very close to their ministers. As a result, senior preparatory committees not only exercise a strong influence, they also tend to over-emphasise the prevalence of sectoral interests to the detriment of policy coherence. Our proposal is therefore to appoint PCD observers to take part in their meetings. These observers would report not only to CODEV, but as well to Coreper II directly and even to the GAERC when significant issues are at stake. To avoid sensitivities over competences, the PCD observers will need to have an independent status (i.e. not be linked to any of the member states or any of the sectoral interests). Moreover, in order to have sufficient leverage, they need to be of a rather senior level (e.g. former diplomats or politicians). At a minimum, they would need to be present in the Art. 133 Committee, the SCA and the COPS (Comité de politique et sécurité/Political and Security Committee), and consideration should be given to installing them in the Strategic Committee on Immigration, Frontiers and Asylum (SCIFA), the HLWG on Migration, the EU Scientific and Technical Research Committee (CREST) and Employment Committee.

4. Council Secretariat to remind of Council Conclusions on PCD

The Council Secretariat is expected to act in politically neutral way so as to inspire complete confidence by the EU member states, and it would therefore be inappropriate for Council Secretariat staff to emphasise a specific viewpoint, such as a more explicit integration of development concerns into a policy under consideration. Nevertheless, when a file could have potential impact on developing countries, it is the Council Secretariat's responsibility to refer to relevant Council Conclusions on PCD during the negotiations and before adoption of any decision. In order to ensure that this task receives explicit priority, we suggest that the Council Secretariat and its Legal Service periodically and publicly report to Coreper and the GAERC on efforts put in place internally to ensure that relevant Conclusions and Decisions on PCD are respected in all the Council's activities and outputs.

5. Strengthen Capacity in the Commission for PCD

Although increased attention is being paid to development issues, we have identified several instances where insufficient attention was given in the drafting stage of proposals and during the inter-service consultation and impact assessment processes. Therefore we propose a substantial increase of skilled staff to pursue PCD objectives in the European Commission, and in particular in DG Development. Their function would be to keep relevant bodies in the Council and the expert groups informed about development implications.

6. Impose a PCD assessment in comitology committees

In many policy areas, detailed implications of EU directives and regulations are shaped by technical committees and expert groups chaired by the Commission. It is often within these groups, composed of member state representatives, that problems with the implementation of directives are first encountered and they therefore serve as an important informal catalyst for policy change. The problem, however, is that these committees primarily focus on the technical aspects of a measure without placing it in a broader policy context, let alone look into its implications for developing countries. But it can happen that a technical committee's decision pre-empts policies that would have been decided otherwise through co-decision. We propose that all decisions with external implications (including all decisions with implications for access to the EU's internal market), notably in the 12 policy areas that have been identified by the Council Conclusions, should be notified to DG Development (European Commission) and to the (newly installed) Expert Groups on PCD. To make such a system enforceable, any decision made in comitology committees in the 12 policy areas must be investigated by the European Commission for any possible impact on development. The subsequent written assessment would then be circulated within DG Development.

7.2 Specific recommendations for improving the potential for PCD in the Council's policy-making processes

Below we specify more specific recommendations, or courses of action. We distinguish between immediate and longer-term action, acknowledging that the latter will require more complex structural changes.

For immediate action

Council of the EU

1. The EU presidency should use its power for assigning files to the appropriate Council formation, irrespective of where the file has been handled in the European Commission (the study has shown that it matters for PCD which Council formation is responsible).

2. When PCD-related issues of significant political weight are at stake, the presidency should consider establishing a 'Friends of the Presidency group' to handle a file in a genuinely cross-cutting way.

3. The GAERC should better utilise its coordination role within the Council with regard to PCD and be actively engaged in all 12 policy areas listed in the Council Conclusions on PCD. It should particularly ensure that the bi-annual PCD Work Programme is of sufficient substance before adoption and ensure its implementation afterwards.

4. Council formations dealing with issues covered by the PCD Council conclusions should report periodically and publicly to the GAERC on how PCD has been taken into account in relevant decisions. For instance, these reports should coincide with GAERC discussions on the PCD Work Programme.

5. Coreper should pay more attention to PCD and ensure that the work between its two formations is better coordinated, for instance by introducing PCD as a standing concern in the Mertens and Antici Groups, which prepare the meetings of Coreper.

6. Even in cases where the senior Council preparatory committee has resolved most of the substantive points on a file, Coreper should still be in a position to review the file in the light of PCD.

7. Special PCD observers should be appointed to monitor the work of the senior preparatory committees, which have a particularly strong focus on sectoral interests.

8. PCD expert groups should be created to advise the sector-specific working parties and CODEV on the links between non-development

and development policies.[12] In instances where expert groups are insufficiently involved, CODEV should report to Coreper II and if necessary, to the GAERC.

9. CODEV and DG Development should agree that the latter reports regularly (e.g. four times a year) to CODEV on policy proposals and on draft negotiating mandates in the making that are relevant for PCD.

10. The Council Secretariat should regularly and publicly report to the GAERC on its efforts to ensure the coherence of Council conclusions, and hence their consistency with the Council conclusions on PCD and other GAERC conclusions on the link between policies and development.

European Commission

11. The European Commission should offer specific training courses on development implications to improve capacity and skills to deal with the development implications of policy proposals and existing EU legislation.

12. Decisions of comitology committees with external implications, including all decisions affecting conditions for exporting to the EU's internal market, should be notified to DG Development and CODEV (or to the newly created Expert Groups on PCD.)

For the longer term

Council of the EU

13. European Council presidency conclusions should regularly reiterate the importance of PCD in order to give the concept sufficient political weight in EU decision-making. PCD should be discussed in the European Council at least once a year.

---

[12] For example, 12 such groups could operate corresponding to the areas specified in the Council Conclusions. They already exist for trade (the trade and development expert group) and climate change (the developing countries expert group). For some areas, the groups could be combined, for instance alongside the Council formations. They could all be labelled as PCD expert groups to give explicit visibility to their PCD function.

14. EU presidencies should give high priority to policy coherence in general, and to PCD in particular. They must ensure that PCD has a prominent place in the multi-annual strategic programmes that are developed by subsequent presidencies, sponsor presidency workshops devoted to PCD-related topics, include PCD concerns in their external representation activities and use their agenda-setting power to ensure that development implications are taken into consideration.

15. Coalitions of member states interested in PCD should develop initiatives to promote PCD in EU policies. These initiatives could include position papers, conferences, workshops, studies and support of development NGOs that are active at the European level.

16. The EU presidency should actively seek the involvement of the informal network on PCD to facilitate regular contact among development experts to discuss PCD.

17. The GAERC should actively promote PCD during European Council preparations by ensuring that development implications have been made explicit and that those implications are taken into account in the deliberations.

18. Development ministers should be enlisted to provide more weight to PCD via their participation in more meetings of the GAERC, notably when trade and other external policies with development implications are concerned.

19. CODEV should devote sufficient time to PCD and actively emphasise the importance of PCD in dialogue with other Council bodies.

20. The Council Secretariat should give special attention to improving awareness and provide training for officials to deal with issues that cut across two or more sectors, such as PCD.

21. Regular rotation of staff in the Council Secretariat should also be motivated by increasing awareness and understanding of policy coherence, including policy coherence for development.

22. As accountability and stakeholder involvement can be expected to increase with scrutiny by the European Parliament, areas that are currently not subject to co-decision, such as agriculture and fisheries, should become so.

European Commission

23. DG Development in the European Commission should provide sufficient resources to monitor policy developments in non-

development DGs and to strengthen input in development-relevant files where DG development is not in the lead.

24. DG Development should pay particular attention to ensure that there are a sufficient number of officials with adequate skills and authority responsible for monitoring policy developments in non-development DGs and to participate in inter-service consultation and impact assessments.

25. DG Development should be more assertive in promoting the interests of PCD during the inter-service consultation, and not shy away from blocking proposals that ignore the development side. Such assertiveness is important to raise the awareness of PCD within all levels of the Commission.

26. DG Development should consider the Commission's Legal Service as an ally on PCD, in the context of its responsibility to verify the consistency of new proposals with existing EU legislation and the EU treaties.

27. DG Development should strive to make development aspects and possible impacts of all development-relevant policies more explicit in Commission proposals, and to do this in such a way that it is understandable to non-specialists as well.

28. The European Commission should also consider strengthening the capacity of non-development DGs to ensure that policy coherence and by extension PCD is taken into account. Capacity and awareness will depend on the number, seniority and skill level of the officials tasked with policy coherence or PCD.

29. The Commission should incorporate development criteria in the Extended Impact Assessments of development-relevant policy proposals, as well as in other policy impact assessments and evaluations. DG Development should establish such criteria in close cooperation with other DGs.

30. The Commissioner for Development, supported by his or her cabinet and DG Development, should emphasise the development aspects of proposals where DG Development has not been in the lead, as these impacts are not always considered automatically by other Commissioners.

31. The Commission should promote PCD in a more pro-active manner in EU Council negotiations.

PART II. SECTORAL FICHES AND CASE STUDIES

1. Fiche on EU Trade Policy

David Kernohan and Andreas Schneider

1. Origins

The original objective of the 1957 Treaty of Rome was to create a customs union between the six founding members of the European Community. Hence from its inception, what was then called the Common Market became the principal actor on behalf of the member states in international trade policy, with the European Commission acting both as an executive arm but also to some extent as an originator of policy.

At the core of the Treaty was the intention to establish a common commercial policy based on three principles: a common external tariff, common trade arrangements with third countries and the uniform application of trade instruments across member states. This implied the abolishment of all barriers to intra-Community trade and the establishment of a single market for goods and, gradually, services.

While this internal trade dimension constitutes perhaps the single most successful achievement of the European Community, this contribution is primarily concerned with the elaboration and formulation of external trade policy.

The new supranational entity was given a legal personality with the authority to elaborate, negotiate and enforce all aspects of trade relations with the rest of the world. The European Community received thereby an exclusive competence to deal with trade matters. It should be noted, however, that with the expansion of the trade agenda, some issues of shared competence also came to be negotiated in the WTO. The Commission is the EU's main representative in the latter institution, but under more controlled procedures imposed by the EU member states.[1]

---

[1] With the entry into force of the Treaty of Nice, international negotiations on services and the commercial aspects of intellectual property became an exclusive EC competence, in addition to negotiations on trade in goods. In the field of services, some important exceptions were included: trade in cultural and audio-visual services, educational social and human health services, and transport. Also a

Situated in the vanguard of EU external relations activity, trade policy has frequently been the initial external relations policy instrument bringing the EU into contact with a range of countries, including those in the developing world. When negotiating with these countries the boundaries of what the EU can offer are often very much defined or at least influenced by a range of domestic EU policies, including decisions on subsidies and standards in the areas of agriculture, fisheries, environment and consumer protection (Woolcock, 2005).

2. Main Council bodies involved

Once DG Trade has elaborated proposals for trade negotiations, the key Council policy discussions take place in a special advisory committee called the Article 133 Committee, named after the article in the EC Treaty that covers trade policy.

According to the Treaty, the Committee's task is "to assist the Commission in the negotiation of agreements between the Community and one or more states or international organisations". In practice, the Article 133 Committee has the main responsibility for ensuring any necessary amendments on behalf on the member states to the Commission's proposals in trade negotiations. Like other Council bodies, the Article 133 Committee has no formal operational guidelines and works mainly by consensus, apparently rarely resorting to voting. In 2004, the Committee oversaw the work of five expert groups, the so-called sub-committees covering textiles, services, steel, motor vehicles and mutual recognition.

The Article 133 Committee is distinguished from other Council preparatory bodies in that it:

- is the sole body consulted on proposed EU positions for trade agreements,[2]
- debates Commission proposals that are unpublished,
- is strongly influenced by high-level Commission experts and

---

blank restriction on the use of QMV (qualified majority voting) with regard to issues without a full internal competence (i.e. foreign direct investment) remained (Eeckhout, 2004).

[2] With the exception of bilateral trade agreements, such as the EU-Chile trade agreement, where the relevant geographical area Advisory Committee is also involved.

- holds substantial decision-making powers, particularly with regard to the EU negotiating mandate (as national officials will seldom intervene in technicalities).

Once the 133 Committee has amended a Commission proposal, it is transmitted to Coreper I, which then transmits the proposal to the GAERC formation of the EU Council of Ministers.

For bilateral trade negotiations, special committees are established in the Council. In addition there are other committees/groups that discuss trade issues, such as the WP on the Generalised System of Preferences, which agreed the 'Everything but Arms' (EBA) initiative and the WP on Trade Questions which covers anti-dumping and safeguard measures. In comparison to the Article 133 Committee, these groups have a much stronger legislative character.

3. Applicable policy-making procedures

In sessions of the 133 Committee, the Commission's DG Trade representatives present their proposal and assess the requirement for a change to their text following a 'tour de table' of member state views. Since Council decisions on trade policy are made by qualified majority, objections at 133 usually need to be supported by a significant number of members in order for the Commission to amend its proposal. However, the objections of a major member state on a significant issue has been said to be sufficient to prompt a change. Moreover, when the Commission refuses to amend its proposal, the Council can change the mandate for the negotiations only by unanimous agreement.

All EU member states have to sign and conclude (ratify) international trade agreements, which usually implies a vote in the national parliaments. This does not tend to cause much problems, but the possibility means that the EU member states and their parliaments can exert a *de facto* veto when the outcome of the negotiations is not to their liking. The European Parliament is specifically excluded from consultation on international trade agreements concluded under Art. 133. This would have changed with the Constitutional Treaty, where the assent procedure was foreseen for international trade agreements.

The adoption of negotiating directives for bilateral association agreements is subject to unanimity. Also, for the conclusion of such agreements, all EU member states have to agree, as well as the European Parliament, which must give its assent in a vote in plenary.

4. Principal parties involved in developing the policy: Their background and level of seniority

The European Commission elaborates proposals for the content of international trade negotiations, with the initial proposals drawn up by the Commission's Trade Directorate General (DG Trade). DG Trade assists, and answers to, the EU Trade Commissioner and also overseas the use of trade policy instruments (see organigram at the end of this fiche). Before a proposal is presented to the Council, it is adopted by the College of Commissioners, acting by simple majority voting.

The Commission in some respects operates as an 'agent' of the member states' bidding and in practice acts on the basis of a subtle mixture of exclusive and shared competences, across the following three stages in the negotiation of international agreements:

i)   the design of the negotiation mandate,

ii) the representation of the parties during negotiations and

iii) the ratification of the agreement once negotiated.

While the Commission is clearly the dominant actor in stages i and ii, it is at stage iii that the member states can (only if necessary) reassert control with powers of veto.

The Article 133 Committee has no set number of participants and there can be around 50 representatives at its meetings. It operates at two main levels:

- *Deputy level*: three to four national trade officials from each member state; commerce or trade counsellors from the permanent representatives in Brussels, plus two to three trade experts from the national capitals, and

- *Full member level or 'top configuration'*: a monthly meeting of national trade officials from member states plus supporting officials.

As the core trade committee, 133 meets weekly during the 'term' at deputy level and its chairmanship rotates every six months, to reflect a national of the incumbent presidency. While the agenda of the full-member 133 Committee is set by the Commission, its members include senior civil servants from the national ministries of member states as well as the

Director-General of DG Trade. It meets (at least) once a month in Brussels or in Geneva when WTO plenary meetings are in session.

While the Council of Ministers has the power to establish broad objectives for trade negotiations – known as the 'negotiating mandate' – in practice the process works iteratively, with feedback to and from the relevant ministries, with only sensitive or intractable issues sent to the GAERC to resolve.

This implies that if the 133 Committee and Coreper do their work and interact fairly smoothly, these policies can usually be agreed at the level of MS trade ministers in the GEARC without further discussion.

Otherwise, decisions are by unanimous agreement in the Council, but only in the most contentious cases where a major country does not vote will a 'silent' agreement be declared *nul and void*.

133 Subcommittees

Membership of the 133 subcommittees is made up of Commission officials and member state civil servants in a similar manner to that of the main 133 Committee. The Commission's participation is primarily made up of DG Trade personnel, but also augmented with representation from other DGs if specific sectoral expertise is required, as in for example the case of aluminium production.

The 133 subcommittees meet twice monthly and channel their findings back to the main 133 which generally follows the line taken in the subcommittee.

However, after presenting the proposal to the Council, Coreper will discuss any wider financial and political areas, whereas working groups will discuss the technical aspects of the policy proposals. The Commission is then represented by the responsible Director and Heads of Unit.

The Commission, present in the Council, regularly amends the proposals according to the developing consensus. The Commission is generally represented by the Commissioner, the Director-General and relevant Director.

Feedback to member states

The participation of member state trade officials is the designated route for member states to approve trade proposals. In response to concerns that member states were being pressured to approve proposals, a 10-day rule was introduced during the Spanish Presidency to allow 133 members to consult relevant experts at national level. Nevertheless, this is still considered by many as a very tight schedule.

In the absence of formal consultation with the EP on EU policy for trade agreements, the only parliamentary input comes directly from national parliaments. However, given the complex technical nature of international trade issues and partly due to varying political priorities among member states, there has been little national involvement to date. An exception to this is Denmark, where its national trade officials must attend hearings at the Folketing, which has consultation rights on all EU policies, including international trade issues.

Other trade bodies

The GSP (Generalised System of Preferences) Working Party meets irregularly. It met once a week when the GSP regulation was discussed in 2004, but now it meets infrequently. Its participants are mainly national trade delegates, either from the permanent representations or from the capitals, and for some countries, development specialists (mainly the countries with an active development cooperation policy). Implementing measures are covered by the GSP Committee, which is a regulatory comitology committee that has been established by the GSP regulation to monitor implementation.

The Working Party on Trade Questions is mainly staffed by trade specialists and much of its work is done through electronic means as the Commission can adopt provisional measures on the issues it covers.

5. Consultation and approval processes

As DG Trade initiates and prepares further the negotiating positions, it also consults with other services. In particular, it consults with the services that are most affected by the policy. DG Budget, DG Sanco, DG Agri, DG Environment and DG Ecfin are regular attendees, but depending on the nature of the policy, DG Development and other DGs will also be invited to attend.

In practice, a veto can be exercised through voting at the Council and via the need for ratification by national legislatures. Powerful member states, such as France and Germany, still exercise an informal veto at both the mandate and ratification stages, to the extent that the Luxembourg compromise extends to the trade area.

Consultations are carried out at the early stage of drafting procedures, and to a lesser extent throughout the preparation process of a policy. To that end, DG Trade has a forum where it engages with civil society, NGOs, trade and business representatives and needless to say representatives from member states.

Moreover, there also appears to be some difference of emphasis among authorities as to whether trade policy is actually *decided* in the 133 – i.e. actually working *on behalf* of the Council itself – *or* whether its function is technically to assist Coreper. These procedural distinctions are perhaps less important in practice, where clearly opportunities exist at the higher level to reach decisions on the output from 133.

Moving on to the higher level, the Council decides trade issues by qualified majority voting (QMV). In most cases, however, the Council tries to avoid adopting legislation through QMV and attempts rather to negotiate a consensus. There is also the practice of reaching agreement under the 'Luxembourg compromise'. As we have seen, the European Parliament has no say in trade matters and can only give its opinion, via its Trade Committee.

Almost all countries can veto a decision and this became apparent in the recent Doha round of WTO agriculture negotiations, where France threatened to veto the Commission's mandate. The Commission argued that it was acting within the limits of an already-approved mandate, which it refused to alter, implying that France must seek unanimous support for any amendment. The situation was rather exceptional as it is generally thought that some countries enjoy *de facto* veto powers, notably France and Germany.

6. Development policy input into the procedure

To provide expertise on issues concerning trade and development, an informal group has been established composed of representatives from the EU member states and the European Commission. The group reports to (and reacts to questions from) both the Art. 133 Committee and CODEV, even though the relationship with the Art. 133 Committee is closer. The group is organised by DG Trade with input from DG Development and sometimes DG Aidco and Relex (External Relations). It is convened on a monthly basis and has recently focused on the issue of 'aid for trade'.

There is also an informal group that examines the interface between trade, agriculture and development. This group meets only once every six months, usually on the initiative of the Presidency or individual member states and is largely dominated by development specialists concentrating on trade and agricultural issues.

As with most policies, inputs are mostly made at the consultation stage. Before proposals are presented to the Council, changes concerning development policy can be raised by the Parliament and other stakeholders. However, neither body has the right to impose amendments to the original trade policy proposal, as the Parliament only gives an opinion and hence its approval is not required. There is no co-decision procedure in trade policy.

Therefore, most of the concerns regarding PCD in the area of trade policy are addressed by the Commission in the course of preparing the proposals. In practice, DG Trade initiates an inter-service consultation with other Directorates General. It also carries out an impact assessment, but only after the proposal has been tabled.

The Council itself (at all levels and in all of its bodies) can however propose changes to the proposal to include aspects of development. The Commission will then decide if and how to amend the proposal in order to reach a consensus. However, requests for changes have to be decided unanimously by the Council of Ministers if the Commission objects to a suggested change. In addition, the Council can also unanimously request the Commission to prepare new proposals.

It is through the generalised system of preferences (GPS) that the EU provides access to Community markets and additional trade preferences to developing countries that observe basic labour standards. Although the GSP Working Party has been mainly staffed by trade specialists, development specialists attend its meetings and development concerns are repeatedly brought into the discussions. Some countries still mainly defend the interests of national industry sectors, but in the end only a few products remain protected from the GSP system.

At a more general level, an increased number of (independent) studies has improved the awareness and knowledge of the link between development and EU trade policy. With more evidence becoming available and cited in newspapers, magazines and other media sources, the issue stands at the forefront of the political debate, which has been reinforced by developing countries becoming more assertive. As a result, the sensitivities over competences have certainly increased, but, and probably more important, the debate in the public domain has triggered a cultural change at the working level, where development concerns receive more attention by trade specialists, or at least have become more difficult to ignore.

7. Strengthening the process to secure a better development input

The policy-making process in the area of trade can be strengthened to ensure PCD. This action should be accompanied by improvements in the way in which national governments coordinate their development objectives, in particular with a view to acknowledging the implications trade can have on other EU policies.

Recent WTO negotiations have highlighted the need for the EU to coordinate at EU level the position it takes in those negotiations, as it is imperative that DG Trade aligns its position with other directorates general, such as DG Agriculture and DG Development. One EU policy cannot take precedent over another EU policy. The same is true for the new Economic Partnership Agreements (EPAs), which are designed by DG Trade but destined for developing countries and hence should include the goals of DG Development. Given the importance of taking development concerns into account in the early stages of thinking about new proposals, one could consider the establishment of project groups composed at a minimum of officials from DG Trade and DG Development, to draft proposals of a genuine cross-sectoral character. This would require also close cooperation at the higher levels, where texts have to be approved.

In this respect, the informal expert group on trade and development also plays an increasingly important role. Although its meetings have increased in frequency over time and its involvement takes now place at earlier stages of the policy-making process, its status is still somewhat unclear (e.g. its position in the hierarchy, etc.), and the topics it can address are limited since DG Trade is very much preoccupied with its competences, particularly in the areas where an exclusive EC competence exists. Therefore, the work of the informal expert group should receive stronger backing by the higher political levels.

The group on trade, agriculture and development should become more formalised as well, for instance by making it an official group belonging to the presidency or perhaps to DG Agriculture and by specifying that it can submit papers to the Article 133 Committee, the SCA and CODEV. The group is currently dominated by development specialists focusing on trade and agricultural issues, but it would benefit PCD if trade and agricultural specialists would participate more actively and would look upon the group as an important source of expertise for their work. When the group reports to the relevant committees, as mentioned above, this is more likely to happen.

Another suggestion for strengthening PCD would be to require an explicit reference to how Art. 178 of the EC Treaty (on PCD) is taken into account in the negotiation mandates for trade negotiations, by including this in the explanatory memorandum that accompanies them.

8. Organigram of trade policy-making in the Council of the European Union

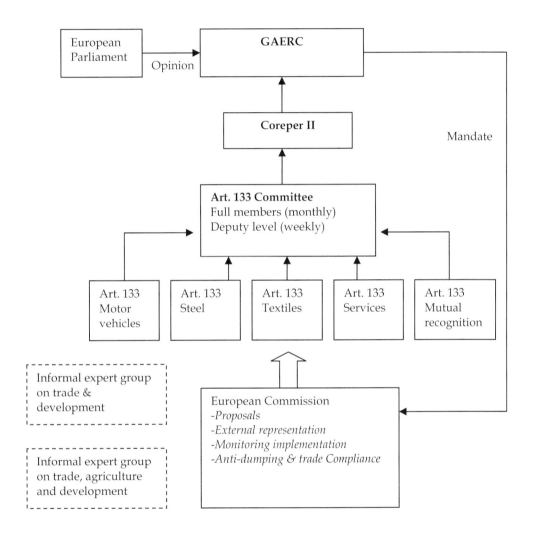

Legend:
GAERC = General Affairs and External Relations Council
WP = Working Party

Case Study on EU External Trade Policy:
Economic Partnership Agreements

Alan Hudson

*The EU strongly supports a rapid, ambitious and pro-poor
completion of the Doha Development Round and EU-ACP Economic
Partnership Agreements (EPAs). ... In line with development needs,
the EU supports the objectives of asymmetry and flexibility for the
implementation of the EPAs.*[1]

1. Introduction

Economic Partnership Agreements (EPAs) are trade agreements negotiated
between the EU and six regional groups of ACP (African, Caribbean and
Pacific) countries. EPAs are intended to promote sustainable development
and poverty reduction by enabling further economic integration of ACP
countries, regionally, with the EU and with the world economy.
Specifically, EPAs are a response to the fact that the EU's existing trade
relationship with the ACP countries, which provides the ACP countries
with preferential access to EU markets on a non-reciprocal basis, does not
comply with WTO rules. There has been a waiver in place allowing such
preferential agreements to exist, but this waiver expires at the end of 2007.
As part of the Cotonou Agreement of 2000, the EU and ACP countries
agreed to negotiate new WTO-compatible trade agreements.

The process of negotiating EPAs began in 2002, with the Council
providing the Commission with a mandate to negotiate on behalf of the
EU.[2] A first stage of negotiations was between the EU and all the ACP
countries. A second stage of negotiations has been proceeding between the
EU and each of the six regions, concerning in particular questions of
regional integration. A third stage, which commenced in late 2005 and early
2006, is between each of the regions and the EU, and relates to questions of

---

[1] European Consensus on Development, December 2005, para 36 – 14820/05.

[2] Council Conclusions on Economic Partnership Agreements with ACP countries
and regions, 13 May 2002; see also Commission recommendation for a Council
Decision authorising the Commission to negotiate Economic Partnership
Agreements with the ACP countries and regions – SEC (2002) 351 Final.

market access. No EPAs have been agreed as yet, but they are scheduled to be concluded by the end of 2007.

2. Implications for development

Throughout the process of negotiating EPAs, there has been a lively debate amongst EU institutions, member states, NGOs and ACP countries about whether or not the development dimension has been given sufficient prominence. The Commission has consistently insisted that EPAs are first and foremost a tool for development. But a range of other stakeholders has voiced a number of concerns about the development implications of EPAs. These include: concerns that EPAs might hinder rather than encourage regional integration of ACP countries; concerns about the loss of tariff revenues ACP countries will suffer as a result of trade (tariff) liberalisation; and, concerns about the impact on vulnerable ACP economies of entering into what amounts to free trade agreements with the EU.

The developmental implications of EPAs will depend very much on how the negotiations proceed and how well they are implemented by both the ACP and EU. If the EU takes into account the concerns of the ACP countries and others, then EPAs may prove to be a useful tool for development. If the concerns of the ACP countries are ignored – for instance relating to their ability to decide when to liberalise, based on their development needs – then EPAs may not deliver the developmental benefits that the Commission argues they hold.

3. EU (Council) players, processes and development inputs

The General Affairs and External Relations Council provided the Commission with a mandate to negotiate EPAs in June 2002. This followed a period of intensive negotiations between the Commission's DGs, and some consultation between the Commission and member states. Once negotiated, each EPA will have to be ratified by the Council, and signed by those ACP states which are party to the agreement.

Within the Commission, DG Trade is very much in the lead. DG Development's role has been confined largely to dealing with the provision of technical and financial assistance to ACP countries. While DG Development has become more active and monthly meetings between DG Trade and DG Development have been instituted, there is reportedly a big gap between these two DGs, with the latter making little policy input, both because it has limited its role, and because of the dominance of the former. DG TAXUD leads on some of the detail about rules of origin, and DG SANCO provides input on sanitary and phyto-sanitary standards. Communication between all the DGs involved is facilitated by an EPA task force – the Inter-Service Consultation – which is chaired by DG Trade.

The ACP countries have found negotiating with the Commission rather confusing; they have assumed that their DG Trade counterparts are speaking on behalf of the whole Commission (on behalf of the EU), and have been puzzled to discover that DG Trade is unable to deal with issues such as development assistance. This is particularly problematic because the ACP countries' decisions about whether to enter into EPAs will necessarily hinge on whether or not sufficient assistance is provided to support their preparations for, and adjustment to trade liberalisation.

Within the Council of the EU, there is much activity, with the 133 Committee and the ACP Working Party being the key fora. The 133 Committee, made up of EU member states' permanent representatives and representatives from DG Trade, monitors the extent to which the Commission is sticking to its mandate. The Commission reports regularly on progress to the 133 Committee. The ACP Working Party, chaired by the presidency and made up of EU member state permanent representatives, provides the focus for development inputs into the process. Again, the Commission keeps this working party informed. With the ACP Working Party dealing with development issues, the Working Party on Development Cooperation plays a limited role, although its members were – along with those of the ACP Working Party – invited to attend a meeting of the 133 Committee in May 2005.

The EPA Expert Group is an informal group established under the UK Presidency. This is chaired by the Commission, and brings together representatives from member states (from Brussels and from capitals) and officials from DG Trade and DG Development. It has met twice; in late 2005 and early 2006. It has no mandate to make decisions, but nevertheless plays an important role in terms of focusing attention on EPA issues and in terms of information exchange. In addition, an informal EPA network of EU development officials meets regularly and brings together interested EU countries that are keen to ensure that EPAs deliver on the developmental promise. So far, it has included Austria, Belgium, Denmark, Finland, France, Germany, Ireland, the Netherlands, Poland, Sweden and the UK.

In March 2005, the UK published a position paper about making EPAs work for development (see DTI & DFID, 2005). As reported in *The*

Guardian ("EU move to block trade aid for poor", 19 May 2005), the Commission saw this as a "major and unwelcome shift" in the UK's position, believing that it was undermining the mandate that the Council had already given to the Commission. That the UK felt it necessary to make such an intervention reveals the depth of disquiet amongst some member states, many ACP countries and civil society organisations about the direction in which EPA negotiations were headed. Poland produced a similar position paper on EPAs later in 2005. Some national parliaments (including the UK), and the European Parliament have also sought to scrutinise the EPA process, and emphasise the need to make EPAs 'development-friendly'. In March 2006, the Committee on Development of the European Parliament (2006) produced a report along these lines. It is too early to say whether this report will have any impact, but it certainly adds to the voices calling for the Commission to ensure that EPAs are truly supportive of development efforts. The ACP countries themselves are clearly in the front-line of attempts to ensure that EPAs deliver on development. Their involvement comes through the regional negotiating process, as well as through a Joint EU-ACP Ministerial Trade Committee. Moreover, they will be part of a joint EU-ACP review of the EPA process, to be conducted in 2006.

Over the last year, there has been much debate about whether EPAs are on course to deliver their developmental potential. As a result, the Commission has worked hard to present EPAs as being primarily about development, and it would seem that there has been some progress on this front. For instance, the European Commission (2005) produced a staff working document on the trade and development aspects of EPAs in November 2005, and on 10 April 2006, Council Conclusions were produced which gave a little more emphasis to development. Some progress has also been made with ensuring that the monitoring mechanism – first proposed by Commissioner Mandelson in early 2005 – will be about monitoring EPAs and their implementation against development objectives, rather than solely about monitoring the provision of development assistance to ACP states.

4. Lessons for policy coherence for development

The evolution of EPAs offers a range of lessons in terms of policy coherence for development:

- Development concerns need to be fully integrated into all aspects of a policy. In a trade agreement, the development dimensions go well beyond the provision of financial assistance. Rather, all aspects of EPA policy, including the trade and trade-related provisions and regulations, have developmental implications. Treating development as a parallel track in trade negotiations is not conducive to the production of development-friendly outcomes. Proposals for institutional reforms aimed at promoting greater policy coherence for development must carefully consider the pros and cons of dealing with development in parallel.

- Policy coherence requires intra-Commission coherence. If development objectives are not to be marginalised, then DG Development must be enabled – in terms of resources and mandate – to represent development objectives across the board of EPA discussions, and must not confine itself to questions of the delivery of technical and financial assistance.

- Effective negotiations with developing country partners also require intra-Commission coherence. It is unacceptable for developing countries to find themselves thinking they are dealing with the Commission as a whole, only to find that they are dealing with one part of the Commission – DG Trade – which is unable to engage on questions of development assistance. When one DG is negotiating with developing country partners, it must be in a position to represent and negotiate on behalf of the whole Commission.

- In a complex process, information flows are crucial. Particularly when an issue is being dealt with by both development (ACP Working Group) and non-development (133 Committee) streams of the Council, informal Expert Groups and networks can play a useful role in bridging any gaps. By looking ahead at the agenda for development and non-development committees, such expert groups can identify issues where development inputs would be useful, and ensure that they are produced in timely manner.

Assertions that a policy is first and foremost a tool for development will not be taken at face value. Some stakeholders will doubt the sincerity of such claims, and others who accept the sincerity of the claim may not have the same view of what is best for developing countries. As such, early commitments to establishing independent monitoring mechanisms can play an important role in encouraging a diverse range of stakeholders, with different perspectives on development, to work together.

2. Fiche on EU Environment Policy

Louise van Schaik

1. Origins

Environmental problems are often a cross-border concern and it therefore seems natural to deal with them at the European level. Initially there was no direct EC competence on the environment, but policies were linked to the internal market competence. Since 1992 there is a separate environment chapter in the treaties and it is estimated that currently 200 to 300 pieces of legislation are in place covering environmental issues. Because competence is shared, in addition, there are numerous national environmental laws. Over time the focus of environmental policies has shifted from direct measures to reduce pollution to ensuring integration of environmental concerns into other policies of the EU, often under the heading of 'sustainability'.

The general framework for environmental policy-making until 2012 is provided for in the Sixth Environmental Action Programme. It contains the development of seven thematic strategies: i) air pollution, ii) prevention & recycling of waste, iii) protection & conservation of the marine environment, iv) soil, v) sustainable use of pesticides, vi) sustainable use of resources and vii) the urban environment. In addition it identifies four priority areas: i) climate change, ii) nature & biodiversity, iii) environment & health and iv) resources & waste. Proposals for EC environmental legislation are drafted by the European Commission. Most of them take the form of directives and regulations.

EU positions for Multilateral Environmental Agreements (MEAs) are usually drafted by the EU presidency, often with assistance of the Council Secretariat. Only for issues where the EC has an exclusive competence (mainly trade-related matters) may the Commission draft a negotiations mandate that is to be approved by the Council. The EC and the EU member states have signed or are Party to 55 international environmental agreements, conventions and protocols.[1]

2. Main Council bodies involved

Although the environment formation of the Council of Ministers is usually in the lead on environmental policy-making, sometimes other Council formations are also involved, for instance with regard to the environmental dimension of the Lisbon strategy (e.g. Competitiveness Council) or the EU's Sustainable Development Strategy (e.g. GAERC Council). The European Council becomes involved in some horizontal, highly political and strategic issues, including competitiveness and environment, sustainable development and climate change.

Environmental legislation for the internal market

Proposals for legislation are discussed in the Working Party on the Environment (WP ENV), which meets often (2-3 times a week), but with different issues on its agenda. Its participants are usually environment attachés of the permanent representations, sometimes seconded by officials from national ministries (mainly environment). Coreper I functions as the clearinghouse between the WP and the Council.

International environmental issues

The international side is covered by the Working Party on International Environment Issues (IEI). It is actually divided into several different formations, each focusing on different international environmental issues:

- *Global*, to prepare for UNEP (United Nations Environment Programme) and CSD (Commission on Sustainable Development) meetings and otherwise to discuss horizontal international environmental matters. Meets about once a month.
- *Climate Change*, to prepare for international climate negotiations (see fiche on climate change). Meets once or twice a month.
- *Biodiversity*. Meets about once a month.

---

[1] For an overview, see http://europa.eu.int/comm/environment/international_issues/pdf/agreements_en.pdf

- *Biosafety*. Meets about once every two months (sometimes combined with biodiversity).

- *Chemicals*. Meets about once a month.

- *Aarhus*, on the Aarhus Convention on Access to Information, Public Participation in Decision-Making and Access to Justice in Environmental Matters. Meets irregularly.

Also for the Working Party IEI (International Environmental Issues), Coreper I is the official interlocutor with the Environment Council of Ministers. However, since IEI meetings are usually not attended by attaches from the permanent representations, who brief the deputy permanent representatives participating in Coreper I, work is usually forwarded from IEI WP to the Environment WP and presented there by the presidency.

During international environmental negotiations, the EU delegates gather in daily EU coordination meetings. In these 'Council meetings at location', representatives of the member states and the European Commission at senior official or ministerial level decide how to adjust the EU position to reach agreement with negotiating opponents.

Friends of the Presidency group for Sustainable Development

A novelty, in terms of organising tasks inside the Council, were the preparations for the June 2006 European Council discussions on the EU's renewed Sustainable Development strategy. These are being prepared by a specifically-established 'Friends of the Presidency' group in which all sectoral interests are represented (see point 6 as well). The EU presidency has also asked all Council formations to answer questions regarding the Sustainable Development Strategy and some Council formations to answer specific questions. In the past, preparations on sustainable development discussions in the European Council were mainly prepared through the Environment Council and its subordinate bodies with some limited input by other Council formations (e.g. Competitiveness or GAERC), which had taken up the issue on their initiative.

3. Applicable policy-making procedures

Environmental legislation is subject to the co-decision procedure with QMV used as the voting rule in the Council. There are exceptions, however, for which consultation with unanimity applies (mentioned in Art. 175):

- Provisions primarily of a fiscal nature;
- Measures affecting: i) town and country planning, ii) quantitative management of water resources or affecting, directly or indirectly, the availability of those resources, and iii) land use, with the exception of waste management; and
- Measures significantly affecting a member state's choice between different energy sources and the general structure of its energy supply.

The EU positions used for the negotiations in Multilateral Environment Agreements (MEAs) are adopted by consensus reflecting the member states' individual competence to negotiate in international bodies and to conclude international agreements.[2] However, in the exceptional cases where there is an exclusive EC competence the Commission is given the right to propose a negotiations' mandate, which can be decided upon by QMV.

MEAs have to be ratified by both the EC and the EU member states. On behalf of the EC, the Commission drafts a proposal for conclusion of the agreement, which is subsequently subject to approval by the EU Council of Ministers by QMV and to a vote of the European Parliament. Given that the EP vote falls under the consultation procedure, the resulting 'opinion' can be put aside by a unanimous decision of the EU Council.[3] The member states have their own ratification procedure, sometimes with and sometimes without a vote in the parliament.

4. Principal parties involved in developing the policy: Background and level of seniority

Several parties monitor the development of EU environmental policies closely. In the Commission, proposals for environmental legislation are

---

[2] The legal basis is Art. 174 §4 of the environment chapter of the EC Treaty. It refers to Art. 300 (TEC), which states that with regard to Community policies it is the Commission that will be authorised by the Council to negotiate international agreements with third countries. The last sentence of Art. 174 §4 stipulates, however, that "the previous subparagraph shall be without prejudice to member states' competence to negotiate in international bodies and to conclude international agreements".

[3] This would change if the Constitutional Treaty would enter into force (see Van Schaik & Egenhofer, 2005).

drafted by DG Environment. Other services follow environmental dossiers closely, such as DGs TREN, ENTREPRISE, DEVELOPMENT and RELEX, with many intense battles being fought during the inter-service consultation (e.g. on REACH). Moreover, the Commission chairs several comitology committees, which have been delegated authority from the Council to oversee and decide upon specific issues of environmental directives and regulations. Given that these committees are usually the first political arena where problems over current legislation are being discussed, they often play an important informal role in catalysing legislative change. Examples of important committees in environmental policy-making are the Art. 19 committee on the pollutants (registration of emissions, waste), the NOx committee, the chemicals committee and the waste committee.

The Environment WP is usually staffed by attachés from the Permanent Representations seconded by national officials with expertise on the issue being discussed. The IEI WP is staffed primarily by national officials. Input is usually coordinated with and monitored by various national interests (energy, agriculture, development, etc.) at the national level. Diplomats from permanent representations usually do not attend international environmental negotiations.

The participants of the Friends of the Presidency group that has been established to prepare the discussions in the June 2006 European Council are cross-sectoral delegations from the EU member states, often seconded by staff from the permanent representations.

In the European Parliament, the Environment Committee is in the lead position. Its activities on climate change are usually closely monitored by the Committee on Industry, Research and Energy and to a lesser extent by the Committee on Foreign Affairs and other committees. The EP's influence is clearly felt when legislation under the co-decision procedure is concerned. Usually environmental policy is subject to intense lobbying, with the MEPs being the main target. In this respect, it can be a real challenge for a rapporteur to bring a file to a successful ending.

The EP's role is less significant with regard to the EU position for the MEAs, where the consultation procedure applies. MEPs are not allowed to attend the EU coordination meetings at the international negotiations.

A key actor is the EU presidency, especially in these international negotiations, where it is the EU's main representative usually in the context of the 'troika' (presidency, incoming presidency, the Commission and the Council Secretariat).[4] In fact, in most environmental negotiations, the EU presidency is in the lead with the exception of the ones that are clearly trade-related and bilateral agreements. In these, the Commission is in the lead since there is a clear EC competence. The presidency also usually prepares the first draft of the EU position either specified in the Council conclusions or in undisclosed documents. In the negotiations the lead representative of the EU usually speaks on behalf of the EU member states and the EC on the basis of what has been agreed upon in the mandate from Council meetings or the EU coordination at the international negotiations (see above).

5. Consultation and approval processes

DG Environment appears to be the champion of stakeholder consultation meetings in Brussels. It is very keen on creating legitimacy and broad support (by environmental NGOs, industry, academic experts and other stakeholders) for its policy proposals. There are also regular meetings with these groups, the most important of which are from the environment side: the European Environmental Bureau (EEB), WWF, Greenpeace and Friends of the Earth, and from the industry side: UNICE, International Chamber of Commerce, American Chamber of Commerce, as well as many sector-specific associations and individual companies.

Environmental legislation – apart from the exceptions that do not go through co-decision – depends upon the support for proposals of a simple majority in the College of Commissioners, a simple majority in the EP and a qualified majority in the Council. On the international side, it takes an active presidency and support by all EU member states.

The Economic and Social Committee (ECOSOC) and the Committee of the Regions (COR) are consulted on all environmental policies and laws (according to Art. 175 of the EC Treaty).

---

[4] The role of the troika is not legally defined. Legally speaking, the troika only exists in the common foreign and security policy of the EU.

6. Development policy input into the procedure

Development inputs into EU decision-making on environmental issues are made mainly at the national level when development and environment ministries coordinate the national position for Council meetings. Also (development and environment) NGOs and researchers emphasise the importance of sustainable development. The European Commission has been particularly active with regard to the World Summit on Sustainable Development that was organised in Johannesburg in 2002. It published a Communication on the external dimension of Sustainable Development (2002/82). The development component also received considerable attention in a Communication in the aftermath of the Johannesburg Summit, which covered the EU's implementation strategy with regard to the commitments made (2003/829).

To ensure the integration of environmental concerns into international development cooperation,[5] a manual was developed in the context of a Communication on integrating sustainable development into Community cooperation policy. The focus is on integrating environmental concerns in development policy-making and not the other way around. In developing countries, however, there is often a suspicion that the EU's environmental policies are used as a trade barrier, particularly since environmental standards set in MEAs are accepted within the WTO's dispute settlement procedures. Indeed, for a small company in Africa, it might be challenging to comply with for instance the EU's packaging obligations. Another example is the EU's stance on GMOs, which have led African states to refuse food aid from the US since it could not or did not want to guarantee the aid to be GMO-free and accepting it into the country would jeopardise its export position vis-à-vis the EU (Ochs & Schaper, 2004).

As mentioned earlier, at the time of writing, the EU's sustainability development strategy is subject to a review culminating at the European Council in June 2006. This is an issue clearly of both environmental and development concern. In the friends of the presidency group that has been established, both interests are represented together with other interests. In addition, the UK Presidency has asked all Council formations to provide

---

[5] See http://europa.eu.int/scadplus/leg/en/lvb/l28114.htm.

input. In our view, this is a good example of how policy coherence could be enhanced by an institutional solution at the Council level. It would not seem feasible, however, to install such groups for many other environmental issues that are less horizontal of character.

Finally it deserves mentioning that the agenda-setting in MEAs is often highly influenced by the EU, as well as the launch of new international negotiations on environmental subjects. Although the commitments made usually incur an extra administrative burden for developing country governments, they quite often as well have positive effects for the health and living conditions of inhabitants of developing countries. In that respect they can be considered a positive contribution to development cooperation activities.

7. Strengthening the process to secure a better development input

In general, the experience is that development aspects are sufficiently taken into account in environmental policy-making of the EU. This 'mainstreaming' has been spurred by the extensive consultation of DG Environment on new proposals and is likely to be strengthened inter alia by the recent installation of the Friend of the Presidency group to prepare the issue of sustainable development.

Development experts have focused foremost on capacity-building as well as budgetary aspects of EU environmental legislation and commitments in MEAs. The requirements as such and their implementation have received somewhat less attention, especially as these issues are considered to belong to the domain of the environment officials. For products mainly imported from developing countries, however, it would seem justifiable to involve development experts. With their knowledge of administrative capacities of the producer countries, they could assist with designing and monitoring the standards in such a way that it would be possible for developing countries to comply with them.

For the internal market, such standards are quite often set in comitology committees. EU member states and the Commission could consider improving their monitoring of which standards are decided upon in which committees, what potential effects these have on developing countries and, where relevant, could take a more active stance in ensuring that the development aspect is taken account of in the decisions taken.

For the MEAs, it would seem important that both development and environment experts are always involved in their negotiation. CODEV could also consider sending an (informal) representative to the meetings of the Working Party on International Environmental Issues (WP IEI) to monitor how development aspects are taken into account in the mandates for international negotiations (both those taking place in Brussels as those taking place alongside the international negotiations).

8. Organigram – Environmental Policy-Making in the European Union with a focus on the Council

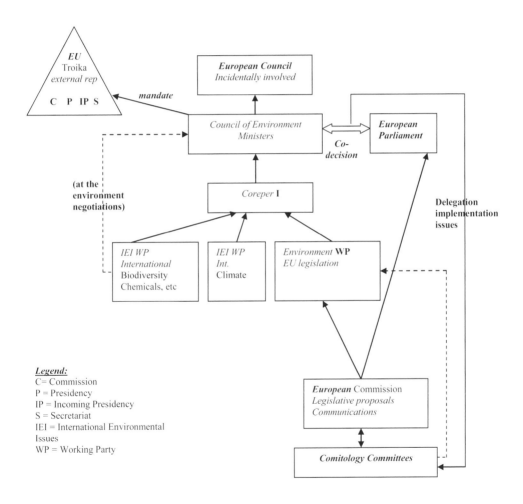

3. Fiche on EU Climate Change Policy

Louise van Schaik

1. Origins

EU policies. As climate change is an area of shared competence, there are both climate change policies at the EU level and at the member state level. At the EU level, climate change is one of the four priority areas under the Sixth Environmental Action Programme that was decided upon in 2001 and which provides a general framework for environmental policy-making until 2012. Proposals for EU climate change policies, the so-called 'common and co-ordinated policies and measures', are drafted by the European Commission. Most of them originate from the European Climate Change Programme (ECCP) and take the form of directives and regulations. The ECCP is composed of several groups, one of which focuses on adaptation to climate change, an issue with high relevance for developing countries. Sometimes problems encountered with the implementation of a directive are also dealt with in the climate change committee that has been delegated authority to decide upon technical details of legislative acts ('comitology system').

International pressure. Since the mid-1980s when scientific findings clearly indicated the likelihood of emerging and negative impacts on the climate due to human behaviour, the issue of climate change has been an important political topic.[1] Its 'public good' character – i.e. it does not matter where on earth greenhouse gas emissions are emitted – led to discussions at the UN level which culminated in the signing of the United Nations Framework Convention on Climate Change (UNFCCC) in 1992 and the Kyoto Protocol in 1997. In both agreements, the EU takes an active part and the greenhouse gas reduction targets set in the Kyoto Protocol provide an important guidance for internal policy-making. The position for the international climate change negotiations, as stipulated in the EU Council

---

[1] In this respect, the first report of the UN-sponsored Intergovernmental Panel on Climate Change (IPCC) has been particularly influential.

Conclusions, as well as in EU submissions and statements, is usually drafted by the EU presidency.

Under the Kyoto Protocol, the EC (EU-15)[2] is committed collectively to a greenhouse gas reduction of 8% by 2008-12 as compared to 1990 levels, whereas each of the individual member states also has its own target under the so-called 'Burden-Sharing Agreement', which, with the entry into force of the Kyoto Protocol, became international law. The EC and the EU member states can fulfil their respective commitments by implementing policies and measures and by buying emissions credits from projects implemented abroad or from others countries that are signatories to the Kyoto Protocol and in possession of surplus emissions.[3]

With the Kyoto Protocol due to expire in 2012, the EU's current focus is on negotiating a new agreement for the period post-2012.[4] Preparations for these negotiations are currently taking place within the UNFCCC context and discussions have already started informally in the numerous international fora that have addressed the issue of climate change, namely the G-8, the Commission on Sustainable Development (CSD), the International Energy Agency/Organisation of Economic Cooperation and Development (IEA/OECD) and the World Bank.

2. Main Council bodies involved

Proposals for legislation are first discussed in the Working Party on the Environment, which meets often (two to three times a week), but with

[2] Because the Kyoto Protocol was signed in 1997 – before the latest enlargement of the EU in May 2004 – only the EU-15 have a combined target. Each of the new member states has an individual target, which is on average similar to the EU-15 target. Malta and Cyprus do not have a target.

[3] Under the Kyoto Protocol, countries with a greenhouse gas emissions reduction target (the so-called 'Annex I' countries'), can fulfil this commitment by domestic policies and measures, certain types of projects in developing countries (through the Clean Development Mechanism), in countries with economies in transition (Joint Implementation) and by buying emissions from a country with a target and in possession of surplus emissions.

[4] The EU has discussed its medium- to long-term strategy in various meetings of the Council of Ministers (Environment formation) and in the Spring European Council in 2005.

different issues on the agenda. Coreper I functions as the clearinghouse between the WP and the Council.

The international side is covered by another Working Party, the Climate Change formation of the Working Party on International Environment Issues (IEI), which meets once or twice a month. It prepares the EU position for the negotiations in the UNFCCC – in which the Kyoto Protocol is the main agreement signed so far. Most of the issues addressed by the Working Party are in turn prepared by specific expert groups and issue groups that are formed within these expert groups. One expert group focuses on the relationship between climate change and development (the developing countries expert group). Also, for the Working Party IEI, Coreper I is the official interlocutor with the Council of Ministers.

During the international climate change negotiations, there are Council meetings on location, the so-called 'EU coordination' meetings. In these meetings, which take place on a daily basis, the climate delegations of the member states and the European Commission at senior official or ministerial level decide how to adjust the EU position to reach agreement with negotiating partners. Usually national development experts present at the negotiations attend the EU coordination meetings.

At the ministerial level, climate change is the prerogative of the Environment Council. The GAERC and the European Council become involved in some highly political and strategic issues. At the 2005 Spring European Council, decisions were made on a medium- to long-term strategy for reducing greenhouse gas emissions. Its decisions were preceded by various inputs, including a Communication by the European Commission, Council Conclusions by the Environment Council and a contribution by the Competitiveness Council.[5]

3. Applicable policy-making procedures

Decision-making on climate change in the EU is covered by the Environment chapter of the EC Treaty (Arts 174-176). Accordingly, legislation is decided upon through the co-decision procedure. The voting rule used for the adoption of environmental policy in the Council is QMV, but there are exceptions when a vote by unanimity is required (Art. 175).

---

[5] See European Commission (2005), Winning the Battle Against Climate Change, and the Council documents 6522/05, 6693/05 and 6811/05.

One exception concerns provisions that are primarily of a fiscal nature, which prevented a proposal on an EU-wide carbon tax from being adopted in the mid-1990s. Another exception concerns proposals affecting land use and town and country planning. Perhaps the most important one is "measures significantly affecting a Member State's choice between different energy sources and the general structure of its energy supply". Given that climate change policies are often related to energy-related greenhouse gas emissions, EU member states at times have argued that unanimity should apply for these pieces of legislation. To date, however, most climate change policies and measures have been adopted by QMV.

The EU positions used for the negotiations in the UNFCCC are adopted by consensus reflecting the member states' individual competence to negotiate in international bodies and to conclude international agreements.[6]

International climate change agreements have to be ratified by both the European Commission and the EU member states. With the Kyoto Protocol, on behalf of the EC, the Commission drafted a proposal for conclusion of the agreement, which was subject to approval by the EU Council of Ministers by QMV and to a vote of the European Parliament. Given that this vote was based on the consultation procedure, the resulting 'opinion' could have been put aside by a unanimous decision of the EU Council.[7] The member states have their own ratification procedures, sometimes with and sometimes without a vote in the parliament.

---

[6] The legal basis is Art. 174 §4 of the Environment chapter of the EC Treaty. It refers to Art. 300 (TEC), which states that with regard to Community policies it is the Commission that will be authorised by the Council to negotiate international agreements with third countries. The last sentence of Art. 174 §4 stipulates however that "the previous subparagraph shall be without prejudice to member states' competence to negotiate in international bodies and to conclude international agreements".

[7] Should the Constitutional Treaty ever enter into force, this would change (see Van Schaik & Egenhofer, 2005).

4. Principal parties involved in developing the policy: Background and level of seniority

Proposals for EU climate change legislation are drafted by the European Commission, where DG Environment and in particular its Climate, Ozone and Energy Unit has the lead. Other services also follow climate change closely, such as DGs TREN, ENTREPRISE, DEVELOPMENT and RELEX, a fact that becomes most apparent during the inter-service consultation. On technical implementation issues, decision-making powers are delegated to the climate change committee, which is chaired by the Commission and further composed of representatives of the EU member states. It is a so-called 'regulatory comitology committee', where QMV can be used to reach decisions.[8] The committee and its three subordinate working groups are often the first to signal shortcomings with existing legislation, sometimes leading to revisions and new agenda items for legislation. There have even been joint meetings with the expert groups that are subordinate to the IEI WP, for instance with regard to the directive that links the EU emissions trading scheme to the flexible mechanisms of the Kyoto Protocol (CDM and JI, see also above).

The Environment WP is usually composed of attachés from the permanent representations, sometimes seconded by experts from national ministries (mainly environment).

The IEI WP is composed of representatives from environment ministries at a rather senior level. Sometimes, officials focusing on specific sectors second their environment counterparts or act as the main representative in the expert group meetings.

In the European Parliament, the Environment Committee is in the lead position. Its activities on climate change are usually closely monitored by the Committee on Industry, Research and Energy and to a lesser extent by the Committee on Foreign Affairs and other committees. The EP's

---

[8] See point 20 and Art. 9 of "Decision No 280/2004/EC of the European Parliament and of the Council of 11 February 2004 concerning a mechanism for monitoring Community greenhouse gas emissions and for implementation of the Kyoto Protocol", published in the Official Journal of the European Union, L49/1. These refer to Arts 5 and 7 of the 'Comitology' Decision 1999/468/EC, having regard to Art. 8 of the same decision, as published in the Official Journal L 184, 17.7.1999, p. 23.

influence is clearly felt when legislation under the co-decision procedure is concerned, but less so with regard to the resolutions issued for the international climate negotiations, where the consultation procedure applies. MEPs are not allowed to attend the EU coordination meetings at the international negotiations.

A key actor is the EU presidency, especially with regard to the international climate negotiations where it is the EU's main representative and usually drafts the EU position. In the UNFCCC negotiations, it speaks on behalf of the EU member states and the European Commission. Together with the next (incoming) presidency and the European Commission, it forms the so-called 'troika',[9] which conducts the most important (informal) negotiations for the EU. The presidency and the troika usually operate with a relatively restrictive mandate from the EU coordination meetings (see above). On specific topics in the negotiations, the EU uses a system of lead negotiators and issue leaders, a representative of one EU member state that is responsible together with the EU presidency for maintaining relationship with the international negotiating partners on specific topics (Van Schaik & Egenhofer, 2005). With regard to the negotiation of bilateral agreements in which climate change is the key or a related topic, the EU is usually represented by the European Commission.

5. Consultation and approval processes

Consultation on new legislation on climate change is done mainly at the European Climate Change Programme working groups and through many informal meetings. Adoption depends upon the support for proposals of a simple majority in the College of Commissioners, a simple majority in the EP and a qualified majority in the Council. On environmental policies also the COR and ECOSOC are consulted with some issues being more relevant to them than others.

To arrive at the EU position in the international negotiations, there are debates in the EU member states (to determine their position) as well as in Brussels. For instance, in 2004 the Commission organised a stakeholder consultation on action on climate change post-2012 alongside the

---

[9] The role of the troika is not legally defined. Legally speaking, the troika only exists in the common foreign and security policy of the EU.

preparation of its Communication for the European Council.[10] Decisions concerning the EU's negotiation position are made by consensus. In practical terms, an active stance by the presidency is key in steering things forward.

Input by national representatives from the environment ministries in the Council bodies is usually coordinated with and monitored by various national ministries (energy, development, etc.). Since this coordination takes place at home, there are differences between the member states, some of which have strong oversight by foreign ministries or some receiving little coordination at all (Beyers & Trondall, 2004). To illustrate the sensitivities surrounding national coordination, with regard to the participation in the IEI Working Party, it has occurred that officials from related ministries decided to attend a meeting without informing their colleagues from the environment ministries beforehand.

All climate change policies are subject to intense lobbying by environment NGOs, mainly CAN Europe, WWF, Greenpeace and Friends of the Earth, and industry groups (UNICE, ICC and WBCSD), as well as many sector-specific associations and individual companies.

6. Development policy input into the procedure

From a development perspective, the international climate change policy of the EU is the most important, but there are also some linkages with internal policies, for instance the amount of credits allocated in the EU emissions trading scheme (ETS) influences the demand for credits from CDM projects.

The EU seems to realise that climate change is an issue impacting severely on developing countries. There is moreover a relatively high awareness that (economic) development is the priority for developing countries and that industrial countries should take the lead in reducing emissions. However, the EU also sees an increasing need for addressing the rapidly growing greenhouse gas emissions in the economically stronger developing countries, e.g. China, India, Brazil and South Africa. In addition, it is important to them to maintain support by the G-77/China in the international negotiations. Nevertheless, when it comes to actual

---

[10] European Commission (2005), Winning the Battle Against Climate Change, and the Council, documents 6522/05, 6693/05 and 6811/05.

financial commitments, they are utterly reliant on their financial counterparts and hesitant to come forward.

Bilaterally there are agreements with China and India, which mainly focus on fostering the development of clean energy technologies.[11] At the operational level, there is some funding for mitigation and adaptation provided for by the Global Environment Facility, the Least Developed Countries Fund and the Adaptation Fund. Most resources however are provided by national development agencies that have decided to take sustainability into account and from the international finance institutions. There are also some EU government tenders and capacity-building projects aimed at the least developed countries and undertaken in the context of the Clean Development Mechanism.

In 2004, Council Conclusions and an action plan on climate change in the context of development cooperation were adopted by the Council as a follow-up to a 2003 Commission Communication on the same topic. These have served as perhaps the most evident point at which development inputs were made, as is illustrated in the case study that follows this fiche. In general, development inputs are contributed mainly at the national level when national development specialists are involved in the coordination of the national position for the WP IEI, as well as through the input of developing country expert groups into the Working Party.

Pressure to take development input into account is strengthened by (development and environment) NGOs and researchers, who emphasise the risks posed by climate change to the sustainable development of poor countries.

7. Strengthening the process to secure a better development input

As already indicated in the preceding discussion, the EU's primary focus is to integrate climate change into development cooperation and not the other way around. Indeed, many synergies and co-benefits may exist at the operational level. For instance, the establishment of a local energy system based on renewable energy reduces the need for energy imports and the amount of greenhouse gas emissions being emitted. But there are also

---

[11]   See   http://europa.eu.int/comm/environment/climat/pdf/ speech_dimas_051208_eu_india.pdf

many cases where climate change and development objectives conflict, e.g. when large-scale investments in the energy sector are more expensive when climate change objectives are taken into account. Whereas climate change specialists tend to focus on 'greening' such investments, development specialists argue that developing countries should be free in their choice of energy sources. The EU, when aiming to reduce greenhouse gas emissions, could subsequently decide to provide the additional resources needed to 'green' investments in the energy sector.

National development experts are involved in EU policy-making on CDM and adaptation activities in developing countries, although they are sometimes constrained by a lack of time and must often rely on their environment counterparts to keep informed of what has been agreed in the high-level negotiations between developing and industrialised countries. In this respect it is essential for participants of the developing countries expert group to the WP IEI to attend the international climate negotiations, participate in the EU coordination meetings, and where possible, be present at the most important formal and informal negotiating sessions with developing country representatives.

An area where more mainstreaming could take place is the EU input in international financial institutions (IFIs), such as the World Bank, an issue that has been at the heart of the G-8 process on climate change and energy. As the EU coordinates its position in the IFIs, it would seem coherent to take climate change, energy and development objectives into account along with the insights of energy specialists (see energy fiche). This would require an active stance by development experts focusing on climate change and energy.

Besides international finance, other policy areas of the EU also influence whether developing countries and in particular their citizens will be able to cope with the increased variability of the climate. For instance, the ability to diversify one's livelihood is key, but the poor in LDCs are constrained by the EU's common agricultural policy and trade agreements as they influence to a large extent the choice of agricultural products in LDCs. This complex, but important situation implies that intensified cooperation between development, climate change, agriculture and trade specialists might be needed in order to ensure coherent policies towards the LDCs. This might be an areas for new initiatives, for instance in the form of a Commission Communication, a presidency-sponsored conference or at a later stage a combined WP meeting or even a Friends of the Presidency group (see full report and environment fiche).

A much larger systemic change would be to perceive climate change less as an environmental issue and more as an economic development and foreign affairs topic. Climate change mitigation and adaptation measures are undertaken mostly in non-environmental sectors, notably energy, spatial planning, infrastructure and agriculture, or are strongly influenced by decisions taken outside the environmental remit, e.g. international finance, ODA and research cooperation. It could benefit policy coherence for development if climate change policy were to be approached from a more holistic viewpoint, for instance to be dealt with by the GAERC, with energy, environment and other interests closely involved during the preparatory stages. Acknowledgment of the wisdom of this holistic approach has already been indicated by the decision of the European Council to continue its discussions of the issue of climate change periodically.

8. Organigram – Climate Change Policy-Making in the EU with a focus on the Council of the European Union

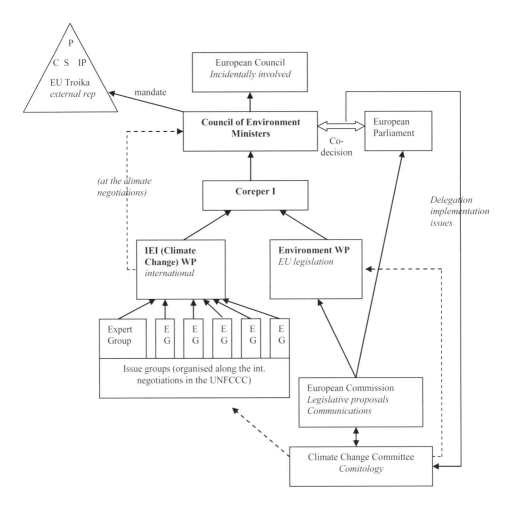

Legend:

P = Presidency

C= Commission

S= Secretariat

IP = Incoming Presidency

IEI = International Environmental Issues

WP = Working Party

EG = Expert Group

Case Study on Climate Change in the Context of Development Cooperation

Alan Hudson

1. Introduction

In November 2004, the Council – in its General Affairs and External Relations configuration – adopted conclusions on climate change in the context of development cooperation, along with an Action Plan. The initial proposal had been made by the European Commission in March 2003, in the format of a Communication. The purpose of the strategy and Action Plan is to mainstream climate change into the EU's programme of development cooperation, and to enable developing countries to integrate strategies to deal with climate change into their development plans, in particular by supporting them in the implementation of the UN Framework Convention on Climate Change and the Kyoto Protocol (see climate change fiche for details of the history of the EU's engagement with climate change issues).

2. Implications for development

Climate change has tended to be seen as an environmental issue, but it is of great significance for development and developing countries. Climate change puts at risk efforts to reduce poverty and make progress towards the Millennium Development Goals. This is because the negative impacts of climate change are felt more severely by poor people and countries, which are more dependent on natural resources and often lack the capacity to cope with climatic variability and extremes. For donors of development assistance such as the EU and its member states, it is essential that climate change is mainstreamed into their development cooperation activities because otherwise their efforts to promote poverty reduction in developing countries may be rendered ineffective. In short, incoherence between approaches to development and to climate change will lead to inefficient use of resources.

The Action Plan provides a menu of options available for selection by the member states and organised into four key themes. The first is about raising the profile of climate change with policy-makers in both developing countries and EU member states. The second is about supporting adaptation to climate change and mainstreaming such efforts into national strategies for poverty reduction. The third concerns supporting the mitigation of the causes of climate change, for instance as regards energy supply, energy use and transport infrastructure. And the fourth is about supporting capacity development; working with the public sector, the private sector and civil society in developing countries, to enhance their capacity to deal effectively with climate change issues.

3. EU (Council) players, processes and development inputs

DG Development, on behalf of the Commission, produced its Communication on climate change in the context of development cooperation, in March 2003.[1] Throughout the process of policy evolution, DG Development was in the lead for the Commission, although there was close cooperation with DG Environment, in particular through the inter-service consultation. There was also relatively good cooperation between development ministries and environment ministries in member states, which was very important for an initiative aimed at mainstreaming climate change (an 'environmental' issue) in development cooperation.

In December 2003, the Council – in its General Affairs and External Relations configuration – agreed Council Conclusions, welcoming the Communication but asking that further work be done by the relevant Council Expert Group to elaborate the Action Plan.[2] In November 2004, once further work had been done on the Action Plan, the Council agreed to adopt the strategy and Action Plan.[3] Climate change tends to be dealt with by the Environment configuration of the Council, but as the strategy is about the EU's relations with developing country partners, GAERC was the relevant Council configuration.

---

[1] Communication from the Commission to the Council and the European Parliament on climate change in the context of development cooperation, 11 March 2003, COM (2003) 85-final.

[2] Council conclusions on climate change in the context of development policy, 5 December 2003. See also "NGO comments on the draft text of the revised Action Plan", EU Consultation Workshop, 14 June 2004.

[3] Council conclusions on climate change in the context of development cooperation, 22 November 2004.

Below the level of Council, the Working Parties on Development Cooperation and on International Environmental Issues (the climate change configuration of this Working Party) were very active. The Working Party on Development Cooperation was in the lead, as it was the expert group the GAERC had in mind when taking its decision in December 2003. However, the International Environmental Issues Working Party was regularly consulted and in fact its subordinate Developing Countries Expert Group was asked by CODEV to take care of most of the preparatory discussions on the action plan, given its expertise on the issue. This feature of the process – involving Working Parties from development and non-development streams – is particularly noteworthy and provides a significant contrast to, for instance, the experience recounted in the case study on fisheries.

In terms of expert groups, the Developing Countries Expert Group was particularly active, informing the work of the Working Party on International Environmental Issues. Its members included strong representation from member states' development agencies, including those of the UK, Sweden, the Netherlands, Denmark, Portugal and France. Relationships between the more development- and climate change-focused Working Parties and Expert Groups seem to have worked well. Indeed, there was much overlap between memberships, with most of the people on the Developing Countries Expert Group also involved in the International Environmental Issues and Development Cooperation Working Parties.

The presidency too played an important and constructive role, with the Irish Presidency pushing the issue forward in the first half of 2004, and the Netherlands Presidency bringing the initiative to conclusion. Under the Irish Presidency the Action Plan was revised through a process involving consultation with developing countries and civil society organisations (CSOs); it should be noted that CSOs had criticised the initial Action Plan for lacking detail on responsible actors, time-frames, target groups, funding and monitoring. The Irish Presidency also worked to ensure that developing countries – the ministries of finance and planning in particular – were part of the process, which will be essential when it comes to implementation. And, the Irish Presidency also introduced some useful innovations in the ways in which the EU deals with climate change issues, making it more outward-looking and more inclined to engage with developing country partners, instigating the practice of having lead officials to push on particular issues, and improving relationships between working groups.

4. Lessons for policy coherence for development

The evolution of the EU's strategy and Action Plan on climate change in the context of development cooperation holds a number of lessons in terms of policy coherence for development:

- The Action Plan framed climate change in terms of development cooperation. This ensured that development concerns were central. It would appear that this developmental-framing came about because of the drive given to the initiative by the Dutch and Irish Presidencies, and the leadership provided by the development community.

- Coherence at EU level was only possible because of close formal and informal cooperation between environment/climate change and development ministries in member states' capitals. No country objected strongly to climate change being dealt with, for the purpose of the Action Plan, as a development issue.

- Even if coherence is achieved on paper by the EU, attaining coherence in practice depends on implementation, within the EU and in partner countries. Involving developing countries – and particularly the decision-makers in their governments – is essential if the strategy produced is to be implemented effectively.

- Effective relationships, and even overlapping memberships between Working Parties and Expert Groups approaching the issue from 'development' and 'non-development' angles can be very helpful for delivering coherence. But, rather than leaving this to chance, when non-development issues are likely to have significant developmental impacts there should be some formalisation of relationships between 'development' and 'non-development' work-streams.

- Presidencies can play an important role in pushing issues forward, and ensuring that development dimensions are to the fore. They can also play an important role in re-shaping institutional procedures, e.g. deciding which Council formation and WP deals with the issue, and allowing non-presidency lead negotiators to be involved in external representation, etc. In order for efforts to attain policy coherence for development to be effective, there needs to be good coordination between presidencies to ensure that issues are taken forward.

4. Fiche on EU Security Policy

Marius Vahl

1. Origins

Security policy is one of the most recent additions to the competences of the EU. Discussions on international security issues began in the 1970s in the framework of the European Political Cooperation. Yet it was not until 1992 that these talks were given a treaty basis, through the establishment of the common foreign and security policy (CFSP) in the Treaty on European Union (TEU) at Maastricht. EU security policy was further developed with the Amsterdam (1997) and Nice (2001) Treaties, particularly in the latter through the creation of the European security and defence policy (ESDP).

Security policy is a primary example of the intergovernmental approach towards policy-making in the EU. The *Council of Ministers* plays the dominant role in all stages of the policy-making process, supported by an increasingly influential Council Secretariat.

The *European Commission,* however, is 'fully associated' with the policy and may for instance submit proposals on the CFSP to the Council – as may any member state – and assist the presidency in the negotiation of international agreements on CFSP. It also manages the parts of the CFSP budget that do not have military or defence implications. The Commission and the Council are jointly responsible for ensuring the consistency of EU external activities. The *European Parliament* plays a marginal role in the CFSP, and shall according to the Treaty merely be regularly informed by the presidency and consulted on the main aspects and basic choices of the CFSP.

2. Main Council bodies involved

While the Council makes decisions for defining and implementing the CFSP, the *European Council* sets out its principles and general guidelines. The *presidency* represents the Union and is responsible for the implementation of Council decisions on CFSP, including the negotiations of agreements with non-EU countries on matters covered by the CFSP.

The *General Affairs and External Relations Council* (GAERC) is the main decision-making arm on EU security policy. The GAERC consists of EU foreign ministers and the *high representative for the CFSP* (HR). Ministers responsible for European affairs, defence, development and trade also participate, depending on the items on the agenda. The meetings of the GAERC are prepared by Coreper II, the more senior of the two configurations of the *Committee of Permanent Representatives*.

Special institutions were established to manage the CFSP and the ESDP by the Amsterdam and Nice Treaties. The Amsterdam Treaty created the post of HR, held by the Secretary-General (SG) of the Council. According to the TEU (Art. 18, para. 3 and Art. 26), the HR/SG assists the presidency. The HR/SG assists the Council on CFSP matters through contributions to the formulation, preparation and implementation of policy decisions. S/he can also conduct political dialogue with third parties on behalf of the Council at the request of the presidency. The HR/SG is assisted by a *Policy Unit*, which operates separately from the 'old' External Relations Directorate-General of the Council Secretariat. A gradual *de facto* merger has been occurring between these two policy-making bodies through the establishment of joint task forces led by 'double-hatted' senior officials and including personnel from both the Policy Unit and the DG for Politico–Military Affairs in the Council Secretariat. The Council may also appoint EU special representatives (Art. 18, para. 5 of the TEU) for geographical regions (the Great Lakes region, Middle East and South Caucasus) or the HR/SG may appoint personal representatives on thematic issues (e.g. non-proliferation and human rights, and others having no basis in the TEU).

A *Political and Security Committee* (PSC) of specially appointed ambassadors of the member states was established by the Treaty of Nice to monitor the international situation and the implementation of agreed policies, and to contribute to the definition of policies by delivering opinions to the Council, either on its own initiative or following a request from the Council. The PSC further exercises "political control and strategic direction of crisis management operations", albeit "under the responsibility of the Council", which may authorise the PSC to take decisions concerning control and direction.[1]

---

[1] See the Nice Treaty, OJ C 80, 10 March 2001.

The PSC is the main preparatory body on security for the Council, as well as being the main body to discuss broader security issues. Furthermore, ESDP operations are managed by the PSC. Formally, the PSC reports to Coreper II. In practice, Coreper II has left responsibility for security issues in the Council to be handled by the PSC. Coreper II is normally drawn in only on considerations of financial issues or where there is a strong Commission involvement.

The *Military Committee of the EU* (EUMC) is the highest military body of the EU and consists of national chiefs of defence and their military representatives. The EUMC gives military advice and recommendations to the PSC, and provides military direction to the *EU Military Staff* (EUMS). The EUMS is a Council Secretariat department attached directly to the HR/SG and consists of military staff seconded from member states. The EUMS provides military expertise (early warning, situation assessment and strategic planning for ESDP operations) and implements decisions made by the EUMC.

The PSC is assisted by two further working groups: the *Political Military Group* (PMG), which prepares the meetings of the PSC and consists of the deputy PSC ambassadors, and the *Civilian Crisis Management Committee* (CIVCOM). Security issues are handled in a number of other working groups and committees, including the working groups on the European Defence Agency, those on consular services (CONON), on rescue operations (PROCIV), terrorism (COTER), the UN (CONUN), proliferation and others. Furthermore, geographical working groups are also involved.

3. Applicable policy-making procedures

CFSP decisions are made in the Council by unanimity. In the case of a member state's veto, the matter is returned to the European Council, which has to take a decision by unanimity. There are provisions for abstention in the treaties, but these are rarely invoked, as they do not prevent the adoption of a decision. Qualified majority voting has been introduced on decisions related to common strategies, the implementation of joint actions, common positions or the appointment of CFSP special representatives. In practice, however, the Council takes decisions by consensus.

4. Principal parties involved in developing the policy: Background and level of seniority

The policy-making process revolves around the monthly meetings of the GAERC, with the other institutions being involved in the preparation of these meetings and the follow-up of its decisions.

The process is typically initiated by a member state or the Commission, or a situation or development emanating outside the Union that is considered to warrant a response or a policy from the EU. The Council or the PSC often request joint papers from the Policy Unit/Council Secretariat on the matter at hand, which is then discussed in the PSC. The PSC then requests a more detailed paper with recommendations from the relevant working group or committee, most often the PMG. Following an initial discussion in the PSC, other committees such as CIVCOM are consulted before the PSC takes a decision.

The matter is then referred to the Council. The presidency draws up the agenda for the GAERC and prepares its conclusions. The support provided to the presidency by the Council Secretariat in preparing the Council agenda varies between presidencies: while some actively seek such suggestions from the HR/SG, other presidencies prefer to manage the agenda with less assistance from the Council Secretariat.

The role of the Secretariat and the HR/SG is nevertheless becoming increasingly prominent in both the formulation and the execution of EU security policy. The Secretariat's support functions are gradually becoming more focused on the HR/SG, rather than on the presidency or the Council as such. Although the presidency draws up the agenda, the HR/SG is virtually always asked to brief the foreign ministers on specific security issues, including the various options for a Council decision.

5. Consultation and approval processes

There are multiple vetoes at multiple levels on EU security policy. To a far greater extent than in other policy areas, security policy is dominated by the three large member states: Germany, France and the UK. When the 'big 3' agree on a security issue, it is highly unlikely that any of the other member states will oppose their proposed action. A strongly held position by a big member state on a specific issue is more likely to sway smaller member states and affect the eventual decision than a strongly held position of a small member state.

Despite the fact that decisions are formally made by the GAERC, in practice most security issues are agreed upon in the PSC. Sometimes issues are already settled in the working groups, typically in the PMG, but more often agreement among the member states is reached in the PSC. There have been a few cases where member state vetoes have emerged in the working groups assisting the PSC, preventing the issue from being brought to the Council proper, and by extension any EU action on the matter at hand. Although the PSC most often pushes issues of disagreement back to the working groups, it does happen that open issues are discussed and even conclusions drafted by the Council itself. This mainly occurs on urgent issues and does not necessarily depend on the political importance of the issue at hand.

The daily engagement of the Secretariat on each security issue provides a continuous push behind EU security policy. Although major policy initiatives from the Secretariat often backfire, the Secretariat has become increasingly influential through strings of smaller more modest initiatives. This situation is reflected in the fact that the number of proposals submitted by the member states have declined considerably, as they prefer to influence the eventual decision through informal contacts with the Council Secretariat.

6. Development policy input into the procedure

Discussions on policy coherence and a 'comprehensive approach' take place at the highest political levels – in the European Council and the GAERC.

Links with development issues arise frequently in connection with discussions on countries or regions with which the EU has extensive development cooperation (i.e. Africa). There is a certain hesitation on the part of participants in the PSC to obtain information on relevant EU development policies. It is often left to committees to inform them about information provided previously to other – more development-related – groups. Coordination at the level of member states also needs improvement.

The member states increasingly ask the Council Secretariat to cooperate with the Commission and DG Development in the preparation of papers and there has been a considerable amount of joint

Council/Commission work on security issues with development aspects, for instance on security sector reform in Africa.

7. Strengthening the process to secure a better development input

The principal obstacle to policy coherence on the security-development nexus in EU foreign policy is the pillar structure of the Union, which requires considerable cooperation and coordination between the Council and its structures and the Commission.

Through the establishment of a legal personality for the EU, the Constitution would harmonise legislative procedures across different legal bases in the Treaty and the procedure for negotiating and concluding international agreements. Yet the distinction between exclusive and shared competences would remain (and thus the continuation of mixed agreements), and there would still be two decision-making procedures – the intergovernmental and community methods – for the CFSP and development policy, respectively.

As long as the Constitution is on hold, procedural improvements are difficult at lower levels for legal reasons. Enhanced policy coherence must therefore take place at the higher political level, either through the European Council or (perhaps more plausibly) in the Council. One possibility would be to increase the frequency and regularise the participation of development ministers in the GAERC.

8. Organigram – Process and structures for the EU's security policy

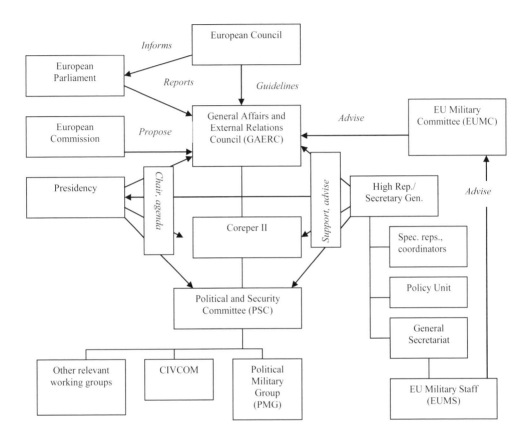

Case Study on the EU Code of Conduct on Arms Exports

Alan Hudson

> *The EU, within the respective competences of the Community and the Member States, will strengthen the control of its arms exports, with the aim of avoiding that EU manufactured weaponry be used against civilian populations or aggravate existing tensions or conflicts in developing countries.[1]*

1. Introduction

The EU's Code of Conduct on Arms Exports was introduced in 1998. Member states retain the power to grant or deny applications for licences to export arms, but the Code lays down criteria and aims at harmonising practices across the EU. The Code of Conduct has two parts. The first is a series of eight criteria, which constitute grounds for refusing an application to export arms, including the potential impact on human rights, internal and regional stability and sustainable development. The second is a set of operative provisions for implementing the Code.

Between the end of 2003 and early 2005, the EU was engaged in a process of reviewing and revising the Code. The process of revising the Code of Conduct is all but complete. Technical discussions have been concluded, but one country has political objections that are linked to the debate about lifting the EU's embargo on arms sales to China. The revision of the Code has been about updating it, expanding its scope and tidying it up. Perhaps the most significant change is that the Code will now likely have the status of an adopted Common Position, and member states will have an *obligation*, although not a legal requirement, to ensure that national laws are in compliance.

In addition, in November 2003 the Working Party on Conventional Arms Exports (COARM) issued the first edition of the User's Guide, intended to set out certain agreed practices and clarify member states' responsibilities. This first User's Guide was intended to unify member

---

[1] Quoted from the European Consensus on Development, OJ C 46/01, 24.02.2006, para 37.

states' practices in respect to Operative Provision 3 of the Code and thus lead to an enhanced exchange of information. Subsequently, the User's Guide has been expanded to include chapters on issues such as transparency and criteria guidance. Criterion 8 – the sustainable development criterion – was the first to be elaborated, with new guidance appearing in the 2005 edition of the User's Guide. Elaboration of criterion 2 (human rights), a criterion that is crucial to development issues, and criterion 7 (end-use controls) is expected to follow.

2. Implications for development

The EU Code of Conduct on Arms Exports and its review, as well as the User's Guide, are of great importance for development because of the close links between security and development, and because of the role of EU member states in exporting arms to developing countries. In 2004, the four major arms-exporting countries in the EU had a 22% share – $4.8 billion – in arms exports to developing countries.[2] Although it is acknowledged that countries have the right to self-defence and may have legitimate interests in acquiring military equipment, there is no doubt that the proliferation of small arms and light weapons fuels conflicts in and between developing countries. Additionally, funds spent by developing country governments on arms exports are not available for investment in development. In terms of policy coherence for development, it would seem inconsistent for the EU to spend resources on development cooperation, while at the same time risking that its arms exports might undermine sustainable development.

The revision of the Code of Conduct and the User's Guide are important from a developmental perspective; the Code lays down criteria and the User's Guide provides member states with guidance on the issues to consider when determining whether to grant export licences. A Code of Conduct with tighter or clearer guidelines about not granting licences that might hamper sustainable development or be used for internal repression in countries where human rights abuses have taken place, may stem the flow of arms to developing countries, reduce the risk of conflict and further

---

[2] See European Council, *Seventh Annual Report according to Operative Provision 8 of the European Union Code of Conduct on Arms Exports*, 14053/05, Brussels, 17.11.2005(g).

human rights violations, and prevent developing countries from spending excessively on arms. Achieving policy coherence for development in this area is about ensuring that the developmental effects of arms exports are taken sufficiently into account in both member states' decisions about granting export licences and the EU's Code of Conduct.

3. EU (Council) players, processes and inputs to development policy

Member states retain the competence to decide on applications for arms export licences. As such, the Commission does not play a role in relation to the EU Code of Conduct on Arms Exports. Rather, it is the member states – in capitals and through their representatives on Council committees – who are the key actors, in terms of both determining and implementing policy through their decisions about whether or not to grant particular licence applications. With regard to the Council, the General Affairs and External Relations Council is at the apex of decision-making, but COARM is the body where the Code of Conduct, its implementation and evolution are discussed in detail.

COARM is chaired by the presidency, and its membership comprises member states' representatives from capitals, a representative from the Commission, along with administrative support from the Council Secretariat. Member state representatives tend to be from foreign ministries; some larger countries may also send a representative from the organisation that processes export licence applications. COARM meets approximately every two months. The presidency meets with the European Parliament once every six months, and, acting in their national capacity rather than as members of COARM, national experts attend twice-yearly meetings organised by NGOs concerning arms export control.

The review of the Code of Conduct, and the drafting and issue of the User's Guide (containing best practice guidelines for the interpretation of the criteria of the Code) take and have taken place through two parallel processes. In terms of development, the action takes place in the elaboration of the criteria. Both tasks were managed by COARM. The review of the Code of Conduct began in December 2003 and was concluded in early 2005.[3] Agreement on the elaboration of criterion 8 passed unopposed in COARM on 26 September 2005 and was included in the User's Guide published in October 2005 as "best practices for interpretation of criterion 8".[4] The process of elaborating criterion 2 – the human rights criterion – is well underway. Germany has led on this process, with a draft now having been circulated by COARM. Subject to the responses from other member states, the process may be concluded during the Austrian Presidency (January-June 2006).

There are no expert groups feeding into the work of COARM; the Working Party itself is where the expertise is to be found. It is very rare for officials from development agencies or from the development side of foreign ministries to attend meetings of COARM, and the Code of Conduct has reportedly not been discussed at the Working Party on Development Cooperation. Yet when the Code of Conduct was being developed in the late 1990s, the Department for International Development chaired COARM and was able to promote criterion 8. As such, under certain circumstances COARM can take account of development issues.

Above the level of COARM is the Political and Security Committee (PSC), made up of representatives from member states' permanent representations in Brussels. The Council or the PSC may issue instructions to COARM. Similarly, COARM's output may pass through the PSC to the Council. For politically contentious issues, there may be substantive discussion in the PSC. Above the level of the PSC is the Committee of Permanent Representatives (Coreper). This committee endorsed the new Code on 30 June 2005; the Council's approval has not yet been given.

With arms export controls, an area of member state competence, the European Parliament has no formal role. Nevertheless, the Committee on Foreign Affairs has produced regular reports on the EU's Code of Conduct, with the Committee on Development providing its opinion too. The European Parliament's report of October 2005 encouraged COARM to further strengthen the Code of Conduct, in particular to ensure that EU

---

[3] Ibid.

[4] See European Council, *User's Guide to the EU Code of Conduct on Arms Exports,* 5179/1/06 Rev. 1, PESC 18, COARM 1, Brussels, 19.4.2006(b).

arms exports do not undermine sustainable development.[5] This report was forwarded to both COARM and member states by the Rapporteur, in an effort to increase the level of engagement between the Parliament and COARM. National parliaments have also applied some pressure to push the review of the Code in certain directions.

NGOs such as Saferworld, Oxfam, the International Action Network on Small Arms and Amnesty International have sought to influence the review of the Code of Conduct, with some success. In particular, the elaboration of criterion 8 owes much to the analysis provided by the report on *Guns or growth? Assessing the impact of arms sales on sustainable development*, although from an NGO perspective the key features of their proposals – thresholds to enable clear decisions about whether arms exports are likely to hamper sustainable development – were not included.[6]

4. Lessons for policy coherence on development objectives

The review of the EU's Code of Conduct on Arms Exports holds a number of lessons in terms of policy coherence for development:

- Perhaps especially on a subject area in which the Commission has a limited role, it is member states that have the responsibility for achieving policy coherence, individually in terms of licensing decisions and collectively in terms of reviewing the Code of Conduct.

- COARM is the key Council committee. COARM has been seen as a technical committee, which is ill-suited for taking account of development objectives. But, with COARM firmly established as the main committee, it is imperative that it becomes a forum where development objectives are discussed.

- Efforts to attain policy coherence on development objectives can be very much influenced by political issues that might seem distant from

[5] See European Parliament, *Report on the Council's Sixth Annual Report according to Operative Provision 8 of the European Union Code of Conduct on Arms Exports*, Rapporteur: Raül Romeva i Rueda, A6-0292/2005 final, 12.10.2005.

[6] See Amnesty International, International Action Network on Small Arms (IANSA) and Oxfam, *Guns or growth? Assessing the impact of arms sales on sustainable development*, Amnesty International, New York, IANSA, London and Oxfam, Oxford, 2004.

the issue at hand (e.g. the EU's embargo on arms exports to China). This can stimulate progress towards policy coherence for development, but also hinder progress.

- Arms exports are a pillar 2 inter-governmental issue, while development is, in part, a pillar 1 area of Community competence. This distinction can be a source of friction, for instance in terms of efforts to prevent the spread of small arms in developing countries. The division of responsibilities between the Commission and the Council needs to be clear and well-understood.

- The use of criteria to guide decision-making about whether or not to grant arms export licences has played a useful role in ensuring that development objectives are not forgotten. Nevertheless, the existence of clear criteria does not ensure that they are interpreted and applied in the same ways by different countries; political considerations can override the application of the criteria. Elaboration of the criteria is very important. In addition, there is a danger that once a 'development criterion' has been established, stakeholders will take the view that the development issues are covered entirely by that criterion. To prevent this, efforts must be made to clarify the relationship between different criteria and to ensure that criteria – which aim at preventing development from being forgotten – do not lead to development being marginalised.

5. Fiche on EU Agricultural Policy

Jorge Núñez Ferrer

1. Origins

The Common Agricultural Policy of the European Union is a common European sectoral policy, where the EU has exclusive competence. The European Commission and the Agricultural and Fisheries Council of the EU are the central policy decision-makers, with the European Parliament only playing a consultative role for the core areas of support. The European Commission has the right of initiative for the policy, monitors its implementation and is generally seen as playing a large role in the policy-making process; its implementation however is in the hands of national ministries of agriculture.

From its inception until the late 1980s, the Directorate General for Agriculture and Rural Development of the European Commission and the Council of the EU for Agriculture ran the policy with little regard to economic distortions, effects on the environment or impacts on developing countries. It was largely considered that the policy was internal in nature and international implications were ignored or misunderstood. A combination of budgetary pressures, rise of social and environmental concerns, as well as trade conflicts caused by market distortions led to radical changes in the policy. Since the early 1990s, impacts on developing countries have increasingly informed policy formulation and decision-making. This is due to an increased awareness that market support interventions and other subsidies can have implications on other countries and due to enhanced attention in the Commission to 'better policy-making'.

The EU's CAP has exerted an important influence on trade flows of agricultural goods, thus affecting agricultural production patterns in developing countries. Production-enhancing support for producers and export subsidies have undermined local production. In some cases, however, the policy has benefited certain developing countries, either through cheaper import prices of certain food commodities or by preferential access of certain products such as sugar to the EU market. However, the negative aspects are widely considered as outweighing the benefits, while unintended indirect development support through distorted world markets is not an efficient policy approach to development.

2. Main Council bodies involved

For agricultural policy, once the Commission has tabled a proposal, the *Special Committee on Agriculture (SCA)*, composed of the agricultural attaches of the permanent representation of the member states, meet to discuss it. The SCA is one of the strongest committees in the Council and is the equivalent to Coreper for most of the files it discusses. It reports directly to the Council of the EU. The SCA often delegates to specialist working groups the analysis of technical aspects of the proposals. There are 22 working groups and 45 associated groups in charge of the specific areas under the SCA, a few of which are related to fisheries. There are specific working groups on each commodity market (beef, sugar, wheat, wine, etc.) and technical groups on issues such as phytosanitary or veterinary rules. Coreper II, however, is also involved in the overall financial and political aspects. Thus Coreper can be found working on the same proposal as SCA, but concentrating on different aspects, e.g. its budgetary implications.

Given the nature of the CAP, with specific directives concerning all aspects of the sector down to very technical areas, the SCA has been less successful historically in reaching agreement before formal discussions by Ministers in the Council than is the case in other policy areas. The decision-making procedure is highly politicised, with lobbies placing pressure on the Commission during the development of the proposals and on the governments of the member states throughout the preparation and negotiation of the policies. Politicians in the Council are also affected by their constituencies, which in some countries include strong agricultural interests. There is thus stronger pressure to maintain the support to the agricultural sector than to support developing countries.

The Commission, however, retains a central role throughout even after submitting the proposal, as it is the guarantor of all agreements undertaken by the EU and is responsible for ensuring coherence between decisions across policy areas also during Council deliberations. Attaining coherence with the separate national policies of member states (rare with the CAP, as it is a fully common policy) will depend on the internal coordination within the member states.

3. Applicable policy-making procedures

As a common policy with precise standards and rules for the different agricultural subsidies and as the standard-setter for the whole food chain in the EU, the CAP is governed legally through regulations. For the regulations relating to the Common Market Organisation (mainly intervention prices, direct payments or export subsidies), the decision-making procedure in place is the 'consultation procedure'. However, for matters relating to rural development, phytosanitary rules, animal welfare or consumer protection, the 'co-decision procedure' is in place. The difference is that with the consultation procedure, the European Parliament only has to be consulted and that with the co-decision procedure, as the name indicates, it has powers to co-legislate in conjunction with the Council.

In the Council the voting rule for agriculture and rural development is Qualified Majority Voting, although the Council tends to not vote formally and to reach agreements based on consensus. Some countries have also historically managed to possess implicit veto power (see point 5). Formal voting occurs in the Council, and the SCA (or Coreper I) performs all preliminary negotiations and briefs the respective ministries. If the SCA (or Coreper I) reaches an unequivocal agreement (usually on non-controversial technical issues), the point will be presented as an 'A point' in the Council, which is usually approved without discussion. In case there remain disagreements, the point will be presented as a 'B point', indicating that the Council has to negotiate. B points, which are generally fundamental policy changes, are negotiated directly by the Ministers in the Council of the EU. The Agricultural Council is known for having the longest negotiation sessions and the largest number of B points.

4. Principal parties involved in developing the policy: Background and level of seniority

The Commission has the power of initiative and develops the proposals. Many consultations with specialists, officials of member states and civil society are carried out during the preparation of the proposals and during the extended impact assessment, when there is one. The Directorate General of Agriculture and Rural Development also consults other services of the Commission which are affected by the policy. DGs BUDGET, REGIO, SANCO, ENV and ECFIN are regular attendees, but depending on the nature of the policy DGs DEV, TRADE and others will be invited to attend. A problem often encountered for agriculture is the lack of specialists in agricultural policy in other DGs, including at times DG Development, reducing their ability to provide input in the policy development during consultations.

Once the proposals have been presented to the Council, the SCA and its delegated working groups will discuss the technical aspects of the policy proposals, and Coreper II will discuss any wider financial and political dimensions. The SCA is usually composed of agricultural attachés or specialist envoys of the ministries of agriculture; the working groups are technical specialists (veterinary, phytosanitary, soils). The Commission is represented in the SCA and working groups by the relevant Director and Heads of Unit. It regularly amends the proposals according to the developing consensus

The Commission's central role is particularly visible at international trade negotiations. Before commitments can be made by the EU in these settings, they have to be compatible with existing EU legislation or if not, they need the support of the member states to adapt EU legislation to the new trade rules. It is not uncommon for the Agriculture Commissioner to attend WTO negotiations and to be accompanied by agricultural ministers from the EU member states who are there to ensure that their position is reflected in the Commission's stance at all times. Top officials from DG Agriculture and agricultural ministries are also closely involved in the preparations.

5. Consultation and approval processes

The main bulk of the consultation is done by the Commission during the course of drafting the proposals. The Commission engages in external consultations on the proposals, with member state representatives, representatives of the sector, NGOs and other civil society organisations, such as the agricultural lobbies, the most powerful and influential of all at EU level being COPA/COGEGA (which integrates many lobbies), or representatives of input suppliers, such as EFMA (European Fertilizer Manufacturing Association). On development-related issues, NGOs such as OXFAM and WWF are very active.

The Council voting rule is QMV, but some member states have enjoyed *de facto* veto powers. The Agricultural Council has often operated under the implicit rule of the Luxembourg compromise. France and Germany are considered in the literature to possess an implicit veto power due to their population weight and importance as founding members and as gross contributors to the budget (Hayes-Renshaw & Wallace, 1997; Nugent, 1999). In any case, the Council tends to avoid agreeing on changes that do not reach consensus, even if it is formally possible to adopt with QMV (Hayes-Renshaw & Wallace, 2006).

The European Parliament is not very powerful on CAP matters due to its sole role as consulted body, while for veterinary, consumer protection or animal welfare, its influence has been much more marked as it has a co-decision power on these issues. The Parliament has an Agricultural Committee composed mainly of MEPs with agricultural interests and who in general tend to defend the interests of the farming sector. Contacts between this group and Committees dealing with trade, development or environment have not always been very strong and their interests diverge. However, a group of MEPs have created LUFPIG (Land Use and Food Policy Intergroup) as a kind of policy debate group on the role of agriculture in the economy, trade and development areas. This group tends to favour reform of the policy and some members of the Agricultural Committee are members of LUFPIG.

6. Development policy input into the procedure

Most of the concerns on development impacts are addressed by the Commission during the preparation of legislative proposals. DG Agriculture is required to consult other Directorates General within the Commission as well as officials of member states and trade associations. During this inter-service consultation, the lead DG has a strong influence, as it decides which DGs to consult and the timing of the process. However, neglecting a relevant DG can cause the procedure to encounter major problems, effectively blocking the proposal preparation. Thus the lead DG has an interest to consult early and widely any proposal in preparation. DG Development is often invited, but it does not always attend or affect the policy development, as either the DG does not have appropriate agricultural experts to follow the dossier, or the officials of DG AGRI and other associated DGs are unable to understand the development implications. It is important in interdepartmental meetings to be highly specialised in the subject and to win other DGs approval for amendments. It is rare for agricultural specialists of other DGs present at meetings to argue convincingly for incorporating development aspects in policy proposals.

The same holds true for the impact assessments, where DG Development tends to be even less involved and less able to provide input in a meaningful and successful way.

For external consultation, the main avenue is a public consultation, in which all stakeholders can contribute. The Commission launches the consultation online with an explanatory document on the reform options and ideas, such as the recent launch of a consultation for a reform of the fruit and vegetable CMO (common market organisation). For sugar reform, a more restricted consultation process was followed, involving only the major organisations, some of which are also represented in the Advisory Committee on sugar. It is the lead DG that determines the scope of the consultation.

Before proposals are presented to the Council, amendments addressing development aspects can proposed by the Parliament, Committee of the Regions or the Economic and Social Committee after consultation. The level of interest these bodies have in development questions has been rather low, due to the composition of the main committees responsible for preparing their opinions. However, neither body has the capacity to impose amendments for the CAP in the consultation procedure, and the Commission is only obliged to incorporate the Parliament's amendments in the co-decision procedure, where the approval of the Parliament in necessary.

The Council bodies at all levels can propose the integration of development aspects. The Commission will decide if and how to amend proposals in order to reach a consensus. The Commission is only 'obliged' to integrate changes into the proposal if at the Council of Ministers a unanimous decision is taken to integrate a specific change. It is clear, however, that sectoral working groups and ministers of agriculture will have a limited interest in ensuring policy coherence for development.

The Council of Ministers or the Council of the European Union (Heads of State) can always request the Commission (unanimous request of all member states) to prepare new proposals for reforming or creating new policies, or to prepare reviews of policies and their impacts, including impacts on developing countries. Although development concerns have not often been the central concern of these requests in the area of agricultural policy, this issue has received increasingly attention since the

1990s, due to pressures exerted by developing countries through the WTO, even if often motivated by the need to find convincing arguments to defend certain measures of the Common Agricultural Policy against rising criticism.

7. Strengthening the process to secure a better development input

There are several areas in EU agricultural policy where procedures for ensuring PCD can be strengthened. First, it is important that national governments have their development objectives carefully coordinated with their ministries of agriculture, given the important implications that EU agricultural policies can have for trade.

At EU level, there have been instances where the positions of the Trade Commissioner have apparently not been well coordinated with the Commissioner for Agriculture or with other Commissioners, including development. In general, it is important that the Commission President not only is aware of the needs to integrate development concerns into the areas of action, but also ensures that all services and the Commissioners integrate development considerations in their decision-making process.

The EU has embarked in the right direction eliminating trade distortions created by the policy in the different CAP reforms since 1992. The EU has to continue this path, but has to be careful that the overall policy structure for agriculture is in line with the needs to assist developing countries to participate and take advantage of the world market. Policy changes, such as increasingly stringent phytosanitary rules which create non-trade barriers have to be avoided. Studies by the World Bank have shown that several of these controls are unjustifiable. Political or protectionist interests of the developed countries, which introduce prohibitive phytosanitary costs under the pretext of protecting human health from highly improbable diseases, should be avoided. An example of the disproportionate relationship of risk versus the costs was the attempt by the EU to impose a standard on Aflatoxins[1] superior to the one required by the Codex Alimentarius. The World Bank estimated that the number of deaths avoided by the new rule was of 1.4 for every billion people as compared to the Codex standards, but would eliminate 64% or $670 million

---

[1] Toxin found in improperly stored cereals, fruit and nuts.

worth of African imports, with clearly more devastating effects on the livelihood of the African populations.

To guarantee that development concerns are incorporated in EU decision-making, it is important to start by ensuring that these aspects are taken into account at the drafting stage. It is difficult to incorporate these once a policy proposal reaches the Council. The Commission must ensure that impact assessments incorporate development concerns, that DG DEV is involved and that relevant experts are consulted. The Commission can strengthen its capacity to incorporate these concerns through training and by having officials in the DGs dedicated to this issue.

At the Council, it is more difficult to ensure that the working groups all follow the development concerns. Officials from member states cannot be requested to follow training on this, nor can the different working groups easily incorporate members of CODEV. There are various horizontal issues – gender mainstreaming, environment, Lisbon strategy, etc. – that would need to be taken into account in all Council working groups. This is the reason why it is much easier to have the Commission integrate the development policy concerns.

In the Council, however, there is at present no system in place for a working group e.g. on environment to give advice on a proposal in the area of agriculture or financial affairs. It would be possible to add one additional step at Council level where working groups on horizontal issues do a preliminary reading to comment on the issue before the sectoral working group convenes. This would require that (specialised expert groups led by) CODEV would screen proposals for any development issues before it reaches the SCA or other Coreper I group.

8. Organigram – Agricultural Policy-Making in the EU Council

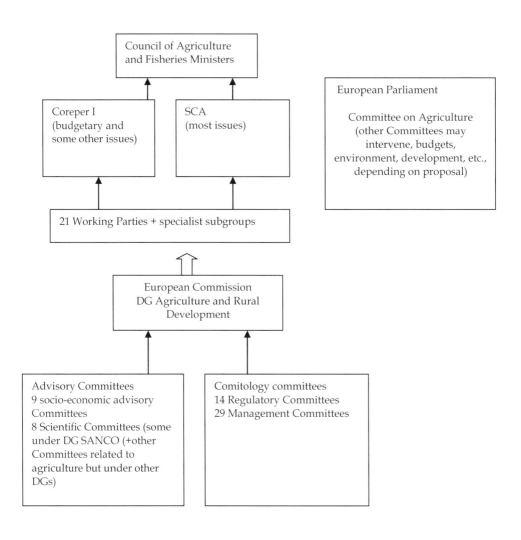

Case Study on the Reform of the EU's Sugar Regime

Alan Hudson

*Within the framework of the reformed Common Agricultural Policy,
the EU will substantially reduce the level of trade distortion related
to its support measures to the agricultural sector, and facilitate
developing countries' agricultural development.*[1]

1. Introduction

The EU's sugar regime has been characterised by high guaranteed internal
prices, quotas, tariffs, export subsidies and preferential access to EU
markets for ACP sugar producers in Sugar Protocol Countries. At great
cost, it has led to the over-production of sugar in the EU, distorted world
markets, and led some ACP countries to be reliant on the preferential
market access which they have enjoyed since the entry into force of the
Sugar Protocol in 1975.

The EU has grappled with the issue of sugar regime reform for many
years, and recently has made determined progress. The pace of change has
increased because: firstly, there has been a realisation that the sugar regime
is inefficient, expensive and unsustainable, and will become more
unsustainable as the Everything But Arms (EBA) Agreement provides
enhanced access to LDC producers; and secondly, because the WTO ruled
that the EU must drastically reduce its use of export subsidies, a move that
strengthened the need to stop over-production.

On 20 February 2006, the EU Council formally adopted a regulation
that will lead to the reorganisation of the EU sugar regime.[2] The key feature
of the reform is a reduction of 36% in the price of sugar over four years.
This will lead to a substantial reduction in EU sugar production. However,
producers will benefit from a voluntary restructuring aid scheme, and
growers from direct income payments amounting to 64% of their losses. As

---

[1] European Consensus on Development, December 2005, para 36 – 14820/05.

[2] Council Regulation (EC) No 318/2006 of 20 February 2006 on the common
organisation of the markets in the sugar sector.

production decreases, so will the need for trade-distorting export subsidies. Concluding a parallel process of policy-making, on 15th February 2006, the Council and the European Parliament both adopted a regulation establishing accompanying measures for ACP countries likely to be affected by the reform of the EU's sugar regime.[3] For the period from July-December 2006, this package of support for modernisation, adjustment or diversification amounts to Euro 40 million, a sum of money which will come out of the EU's development budget. However, none of this will be paid until the end of the year as applications for funds must first be evaluated. Support will continue during the period 2007-13 although the level is still under negotiation. These funds will again be provided from the development budget.

2. Implications for development

The reform of the EU's sugar regime has complex development implications. First, those ACP countries that have enjoyed preferential access to the high and guaranteed prices of the EU market will lose revenues of around €250 million per year, even if they do not reduce production in response to the price cut. However, the likely result of the price cut will be a decline of production in many of the Sugar Protocol countries, so actual losses of income could amount to €500 million per year. Second, the fully liberalised access to the EU market which least-developed countries will enjoy from 2009 under the EBA Agreement, will be access to a market characterised by lower prices than currently pertain. And, if their exports to the EU increase too rapidly, then LDCs may be subject to import restrictions. And third, reduced dumping of EU sugar will enable efficient sugar producers such as Brazil and South Africa to capture a larger share of the world market. The world market price is expected to increase as a result of reduced EU production, although there is considerable uncertainty over the outcome.

The impact on countries in sub-Saharan Africa will depend on what access they have had to EU markets (whether they are Sugar Protocol

---

[3] Regulation (EC) No 266/2006 of the European Parliament and of the Council of 15 February 2006 establishing accompanying measures for Sugar Protocol countries affected by the reform of the EU sugar regime.

countries), what access they will have to EU markets (whether they are EBA, and to what extent future Economic Partnership Agreements improve access), and how efficient their sugar producers are. In general, Sugar Protocol countries will lose out, and EBA countries will gain, but not by as much as they would have done had EU prices remained inflated. Efficient producers will prosper, inefficient producers may be forced out of business.

3. EU (Council) players, processes and development inputs

In September 2003 the Commission published a Communication and Impact Assessment setting out options for reform of the EU sugar regime. This was followed in July 2004 by a Commission Communication outlining its proposals for the future of the sugar regime.[4] The Commission's revised proposal – taking account of the views of a wide range of interests – was presented in June 2005, with DG Agriculture and Rural Development taking the lead.[5] At the same time, the Commission – with DG Development in the lead – presented a proposal for a regulation of the European Parliament and the Council to establish accompanying measures for those ACP countries affected by reform of the EU sugar regime.[6]

As regards the reform of the EU sugar regime, the Council institutions involved have been the Agriculture and Fisheries Council, the Special Committee on Agriculture, and the Working Party on Sugar and Iso-glucose. These fora were the venues for discussion of the internal implications and technicalities of the EU sugar reform, discussions to which, it has been suggested, development experts could contribute little. Certain member states – including the UK – ensured that development issues and the interests of ACP states were raised, for instance at meetings of the Special Committee on Agriculture.

---

[4] Communication from the Commission to the Council and the European Parliament, Accomplishing a sustainable agricultural model for Europe through the reformed CAP – sugar sector reform COM(2004) 499-final.

[5] Commission proposal for a Council Regulation on the common organisation of the markets in the sugar sector, COM(2005) 263-final.

[6] Commission proposal for a regulation of the European Parliament and of the Council establishing accompanying measures for Sugar Protocol countries affected by the reform of the EU sugar regime, COM (2005) 266-final.

As regards the accompanying measures for ACP countries, the key Council institutions have been the General Affairs and External Relations Council (GAERC), Coreper and the Working Party on Development Cooperation (CODEV). The ACP Working Party also debated the accompanying measures for Sugar Protocol countries. These fora were the venues for discussions on the accompanying measures, not least because the payment for such measures would come out of the development budget. Very few member states – the Netherlands, Germany and Sweden – seem to have been willing to discuss the possibility of funding accompanying measures from the agriculture budget, a so-called 'agricultural dividend'. And, with financing to be discussed at ECOFIN, and at the Agrifin Working Party it was difficult for those member states keen to push for an 'agricultural dividend' to make their case at the ACP or Development Cooperation Working Party. There is little evidence of contact between the Working Party on Development Cooperation and the Working Party on sugar and iso-glucose; it would seem that the former focused on the accompanying measures, and the latter on the nature of the EU's internal reform.

The European Parliament was active both in terms of the accompanying measures, which were dealt with under the co-decision procedure, and in terms of the reform of the EU's sugar regime itself, which was dealt with under the consultation procedure. On the former, the Development Committee led, taking the view that the accompanying measures to support Sugar Protocol producers in 2006 – €40 million – are quite inadequate, particularly in comparison with the generous compensation offered to EU sugar producers.[7] Criticisms of the reforms and the support package were also strongly voiced by NGOs including Oxfam who had lobbied hard throughout the process on behalf of what they took to be the interests of the Sugar Protocol countries. The Sugar Protocol countries themselves, along with the LDCs, argued strongly for more gradual reform. The Committee on Agriculture and Rural Development led on the EU's reforms themselves, and proposed many amendments to dilute the reform package, including that of restricting

---

[7] Report on the proposal for a regulation of the European Parliament and of the Council establishing accompanying measures for Sugar Protocol countries affected by the reform of the EU sugar regime, A6-0281-2005-final.

imports from LDCs.[8] However its report, published in December 2005, came after the Council had largely agreed on the package of reforms.

By the time the proposals were adopted in February 2006, the price cut had fallen to 36% from 39%, the amount of income that would be provided to farmers via the Single Payment System was unchanged, and the time taken to complete the reform had increased from 2 years to 4 years.

4. Lessons for policy coherence for development

The reform of the EU's sugar regime holds a range of lessons in terms of policy coherence for development:

- Dealing with development on a parallel track, separate from the main policy proposal, may be effective in terms of reaching some sort of agreement. But when discussions take place primarily in non-development fora, and communications between development and non-development fora are poor, there is a risk that development concerns may not be taken account of sufficiently.
- Coherence at the level of the EU will only come about if there is coherence at the level of individual member states.
- Decisions on policy reform are taken by those from whose budget line the reforms will be paid. For development interests to be taken account of, they must be voiced at fora where those who will pay for reform come together. If financing decisions are taken at fora where development interests are poorly represented, then financing decisions will take little account of development.
- The impacts of proposed reforms can be uncertain, and – certainly in the sugar case – are likely to vary across developing countries. Therefore, it is difficult to say what a development-friendly outcome – an outcome in which policy coherence for development has been attained – is. In a related vein, considerations of impact must be disaggregated by country-type, and all players must be clear what they mean when they say that development is being taken account of; otherwise such claims will become meaningless.

---

[8] Report on the proposal for a Council regulation on the common organisation of the markets in the sugar sector, A6-0391-2005.

6. Fiche on EU Fisheries Policy

Jorge Núñez Ferrer

1. Origins

EU has exclusive competence in fisheries, as is the case for agriculture. The effect of exclusive competence means that member states no longer have the power to introduce their own legislation in this area.

The Common Fisheries Policy of the European Union has recently been reformed first and foremost due to the unsustainable exploitation of Community waters. However, it also addresses the need to improve fisheries agreements with third countries and in particular developing nations. The Community has one of the largest fishing fleets in the world. Most of it operates within Community waters, but an important part of the EU fishing sector depends on access to external resources shared with third countries. These are in waters under the jurisdiction of non-EU coastal states or in international waters. The conditions of access have to be agreed between the EU and coastal or flag states.

The EU adheres today to a Code of Conduct in its international agreements, which includes not only the need to ensure that fishing resources are used in a sustainable way, but also includes a specific assistance package for the developing country partners to modernise their fleet. This is achieved through Fisheries Partnership Agreements (FPA).

Also at international level, specialised multinational bodies and Regional Fisheries Organisations (RFOs) have been established to coordinate fisheries activities. The EU has thus an active international role in fishery resource use and in developing countries fishing fleet development and use. Nevertheless, the actual benefits of the EU approach are undermined by weak statistical data on stocks and the unrestricted bilateral agreements of those developing countries with other nations.

2. Main Council bodies involved

For the Fisheries Policy decision-making cycle, once the Commission has tabled a proposal, Coreper I, composed of the deputy permanent representatives of the member states, discusses these proposals. Specialist working groups look after the common fisheries policy; four are exclusively dedicated to fisheries. For development issues and the FPA, the working group on External Fisheries Policy is the most important.

The Commission, however, retains a central role throughout and even after submitting proposals, as it is the guarantor of all agreements undertaken by the EU and responsible to ensure coherence between decisions across policy areas also in the Council.

For fishing agreements, FPAs, the Commission has the mandate to negotiate on behalf of the member states. The member states with international fleets have representatives present at the negotiations, and sometimes also representatives of other member states interested in the quality of the EU's agreements with third countries.

3. Applicable policy-making procedures

For general policy changes, the decision making procedure in place is the 'consultation procedure', for FPAs the member states have to ratify agreements in the GAERC Council.

The voting rule for fisheries in the Agriculture and Fisheries Council is Qualified Majority Voting, although the Council tends to not vote formally and reach agreements based on consensus. Some countries have also historically managed to possess implicit veto power, because they have major fishing fleets. Countries without a large fishing fleet or access to the sea often do not actively participate in policy decisions, allowing the large fishing nations to have a strong influence on the policy.

4. Principal parties involved in developing the policy: Background and level of seniority

The Commission has the power of initiative and develops the proposals. Many consultations with specialists, officials of member states and civil society are carried out during the preparation of the proposals. For the 2002 fisheries reform, the Commission embarked on a wide consultation process with the publication of the Green Paper on the Future of the Fisheries Policy. The Directorate General of Fisheries also consults other services of the Commission which are affected by the policy. DGs AGRI, BUDG, REGIO, SANCO, ENV and ECFIN are regular attendees, but depending on the nature of the policy DGs DEV, TRADE, RELEX or others will be invited to attend the interservice meetings at the level of officials and sometimes Heads of Unit. See section 5 for more details.

Once a proposal has been presented to the Council, Coreper I discusses it. Working groups will address specific areas of the policy. The three main working groups are: Working Party on External Fisheries Policy, Working Party on Internal Fisheries Policy and the Working Party of Directors-General of Fisheries Departments. The first two are attended mainly by the fishery attachés of the permanent representations. Other working parties are involved in fisheries as well, such as the working party of veterinary experts for fisheries, or working parties on labelling or Codex Alimentarius. The Commission is represented in Coreper and working groups by the responsible Director and Heads of Unit.

Non-controversial items may be agreed at Coreper level and will be presented in the Council as A points, usually technical issues agreed without discussion by the ministers. 'B' points, generally fundamental policy changes, are negotiated directly by the Ministers in the Council of the EU. The Commission, present in the Council, regularly amends the proposals according to the developing consensus. The Commission is generally represented by the Commissioner, the Director General and the relevant Director.

5. Consultation and approval processes

The bulk of the consultation is done by the Commission during the drafting time of the proposals. The Commission engages in external consultations on the proposals, with member state representatives, representatives of the sector, NGOs and other civil society organisations.

As for agriculture, the decision-making procedure is highly politicised, with lobbies placing much pressure on the Commission during the development of the proposals and on the governments of the member states throughout the preparation and negotiation of the policies. Given the rather specific nature of the policy, interests are concentrated on specific countries and interest groups, which has historically affected the discussions on wider policy external policy implications. Nevertheless, the Commission's commitment to incorporate a serious development dimension and the serious interest by some member states to do so, have resulted in important changes in this direction.

The Council voting rule is QMV, but some member states have enjoyed *de facto* veto powers. Generally, the fisheries policy is of major importance only for the countries with large fishing fleets. Thus countries with a keen interest, such as Spain, France or the UK, have a very large say in the policy. Countries with small fleets or no access to the sea are less involved.

6. Development policy input into the procedure

Most of the concerns on development impacts are addressed by the Commission during the preparation of the proposals. DG Fisheries consults internally other Directorates General and externally officials of member states and lobbyists. Impacts on third countries and the developing countries in particular are becoming an integral part of the extended impact assessment now required before any proposal is presented. The Green Paper in 2001 (COM(2001) 135 final) started the consultation process on the future of the policy and dedicated an important part of the document to development concerns. Extended impact assessments were prepared, as required. Development impacts were included in these assessments, although only to a limited extent.

DG Fisheries is required to consult internally other Directorates General and externally officials of member states and lobbyists. As the knowledge in other DGs and DG Development on the fisheries policy is weak, only marginal inputs were made. As a consequence, the wider implications of the fisheries policy are often weakly addressed in Commission proposals.

Amendments addressing development aspects can be proposed by the European Parliament, the Economic and Social Committee or the Committee of the Regions after their consultation, but these bodies do not have the capacity to impose amendments. In any case, for fisheries, due to the very specific characteristics of the sector, participation in these bodies is limited.

The Council bodies at all levels can propose to integrate development aspects. The Commission will decide if and how to amend proposals in order to reach a consensus. The Commission is only 'obliged' to integrate changes into the proposal if, at the Council of Ministers, a unanimous decision is taken to integrate a specific change. The Council of Ministers or the European Council (Heads of State) can always request the Commission (unanimous request of all member states) to prepare new proposals for reforming or creating new policies, or to prepare reviews of policies and their impacts, including impacts on developing countries. How far these development concerns are actually taken into account will depend on the quality of the proposals and the interest of member states in development issues.

7. Strengthening the process to secure a better development input

For the fisheries sector there are several areas where procedures can be strengthened. First, it is important that national governments have their development objectives properly coordinated with their ministry responsible for fisheries, given the important effect the EU can have on international fishing waters. This would notably apply both for member states with a keen interest in fisheries policies, but as well for member states with strong development cooperation links to countries where the fisheries sector is or could be an important contributor to economic development.

It is the Commission that ensures that across all Council meetings, no EU policies and international commitments are in conflict with each other. Coherence at EU level should be guaranteed by the Commission. Coherence with national policies has to be guaranteed by the national representatives at the working group and Council level.

This indicates already that the key point to ensure coherence is to have a strong initial input by the Commission. As an initiator of policy, its capacity to integrate development concerns is critical. The Commission has formal systems in place to incorporate development concerns. Reinforcing these can take the form of specialist training for relevant Commission officials, the existence of a specialist official in the DGs overseeing the work of the DG, or further improving the method of consultation of the Commission, internally and externally. The EU is a very open institution for consultation; thus most changes could concentrate on reinforcing the capacity and improving existing mechanisms.

At Council level this is more difficult. Ensuring that member state officials are aware of development concerns cannot be imposed as in an organisation like the Commission. However, proposals could be screened first by specialised horizontal working groups, such as CODEV, before the specific and sectoral groups meet. This would ensure that the Council participates more fully in the policy coherence process but without burdening the specialised groups with additional horizontal-issue officials, making the Council meetings unworkable. Additionally, since the Common Fisheries Policy is still under the consultation procedure, introducing co-decision could increase the interest of the European Parliament's Development Committee to propose policy amendments.

8. Organigram of Fisheries Policy-Making in the Council of the EU

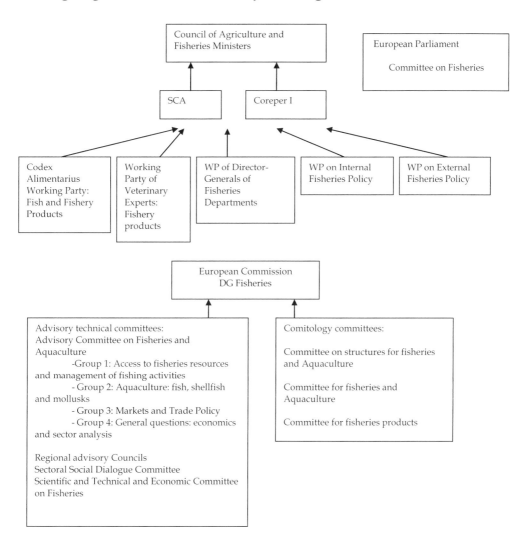

Case Study of the Fisheries Partnership Agreements

Alan Hudson

The EU will continue to pay particular attention to the
development objectives of the countries with which the
Community has or will agree fisheries agreements.[1]

1. Introduction

The EU has, for more than 20 years, entered into agreements with developing countries to gain access to their coastal fishing waters in return for financial compensation. In principle, the EU will fish only where there is a surplus stock which the local fleet does not have the capacity to catch. In practice – because of the difficulties of accurately estimating stock levels, and because short-term economic interests have taken priority over sustainable development – it seems likely that the EU fleet has fished beyond sustainable levels. Some 80% of the economic benefits of the EU's external fishing agreements go to the Spanish fleet, with Portugal, France, Italy, the Netherlands, Greece, Poland and Lithuania also benefiting. By paying financial compensation to third countries, the EU in effect subsidises its member states' fleets.

In July 2004, the Agriculture and Fisheries Council agreed to the Commission's proposal for an integrated framework for Fisheries Partnership Agreements (FPAs) with third countries.[2] Such agreements are an external dimension of the EU's Common Fisheries Policy. The integrated framework is intended to provide the basis for FPAs which, by prioritising sustainable development, will meet the needs of the EU fishing fleet, and the needs of fisheries sectors in developing countries. In contrast to earlier agreements, a portion – between 20 and 40% – of the financial transfer should be for targeted measures to help develop the local fisheries sector. Thus far, no FPAs have been ratified; Morocco's is closest to ratification. All

---

[1] European Consensus on Development, December 2005, para 36 – 14820/05.

[2] Council conclusions on fisheries partnership agreements with third countries, 19 July 2004.

third country agreements which include financial compensation are due to be replaced by FPAs by 2008.

2. Implications for development

The EU's fisheries policy has major implications for developing countries. Of the EU's 20 fisheries agreements with third countries, 18 are with ACP states. For many of these states, the financial rewards they receive from granting access to the EU fleet are substantial; in total, annual payments have amounted to €150 million. For some developing countries, such payments can be a significant source of revenue. But the importance of fisheries extends beyond the payments received for access; in terms of people's livelihoods and their diets, and in terms of government revenues. For instance, in Senegal, around 15% of the economically active population derived their livelihoods from fisheries, with fish providing 75% of the animal protein in the population's diet, and up to 50% of export earnings come from fish products.[3]

If the sustainability of fisheries in developing countries is undermined, there will be high developmental costs and eventually a loss of the revenue from fisheries agreements. Therefore, if the EU is serious about promoting development in its partner countries, then it must ensure coherence between the two objectives of its external fisheries agreements: promoting the interests of its distant-water fishing fleet, and ensuring the sustainable development of third country fisheries. The concept of Fisheries Partnership Agreements goes some way in recognising that sustainable development is crucial, but it remains to be seen how they will work out in practice.

3. EU (Council) players, processes and development inputs

In 2000, the Commission submitted a Communication to the Council and the European Parliament on fisheries and poverty reduction, emphasising the need for coherence between the EU's policies on development and on

---

[3] Source: Coalition for Fair Fisheries Agreements – cited in DFID's "Developments: The international development magazine".

fisheries.[4] This was followed by a Council Resolution on fisheries and poverty reduction in 2001, and then – after the revision of the Common Fisheries Policy – a Communication from the Commission on an Integrated Framework for Fisheries Partnership Agreements with Third Countries, in December 2002.[5] The Council conclusions on fisheries partnership agreements were produced in July 2004, after 18 months of negotiations, a period of time which illustrates the complexity of the issues and the diversity of EU member states' views. By July 2004, near-consensus had been reached, but Coreper was invited to consider proposed amendments from Sweden and Germany, relating in particular to making the results of impact assessments available to member states in good time.

The Council Conclusions of 2004 provide the Commission with the framework to negotiate specific FPAs with third countries. A mandate is also required from the Council for each specific agreement. With fisheries being an area of Community competence, the Commission is very much in the lead. It is the hub of negotiations, with other institutions – including Council Working Groups – reportedly reduced to the role of pleading with the Commission to take certain issues forward. Within the Commission, DG Fisheries is very much in the lead, with DG Development consulted as regards implementation and monitoring, but somewhat marginalised and lacking the resources to be a champion for development issue as regards fisheries policy. Development, it would seem, is not the motivation for FPAs; their purpose is to promote the interests of EU fishing fleets.

The Working Party on External Fisheries Policy is the key Council Working Party on FPAs. It meets twice a month, and is made up of staff from member states' permanent representations and experts from capitals. Discussions on fisheries at the Working Party on Development Cooperation are reported to be extremely rare, a situation that is explained by a clear – perhaps too clear – division of labour between the fisheries and development working parties. And, there have been very few development

---

[4] Communication from the Commission to the Council and the European Parliament on Fisheries and Poverty Reduction, 8 November 2000, COM (2000) 724-final.

[5] Communication from the Commission on an integrated framework for fisheries partnership agreements with third countries, 23 December 2002, COM (2002) 637-final.

inputs into the Working Party on External Fisheries Policy. Indeed, there seems to be little opportunity for development interests to feed into Council discussions of FPAs.

In September 2003, the Committee on Fisheries of the European Parliament produced, on its own initiative, a report on the FPAs' proposal, with the Committee on Development Cooperation also offering its opinion.[6] The former gave more emphasis to the interests of the EU fishing fleet, the latter more emphasis to sustainable development issues. The net effect of these opinions on the approach to FPAs taken by the Commission appears to have been negligible.

During negotiations with third countries, the Commission and member states hold official Council Working Group meetings in the margins, in which the Commission informs member states of progress. Member states with strong interests in promoting the interests of their fishing fleets send their representatives to promote their national interests. In recent years, other countries including Germany, the Netherlands, Sweden, and the UK have also sent representatives to promote development interests.

Once negotiations are concluded, the Commission will initial the agreement which then has to be ratified by the third country and by the European Community under Art. 37 and hence by qualified majority voting. Parliament can give its opinion under the consultation procedure. The Council has not blocked a fisheries agreement; this reflects both the fact that the Commission works closely to the Council's mandate, and the fact that no member state has felt it appropriate to block – on the grounds of development concerns – the progress of an agreement in the Agriculture and Fisheries Council.

The ACP states are of course part of the FPA negotiations, but there are serious question marks about the capacity of many individual ACP states to defend their interests in negotiations with the European Union. The FPAs may be a step towards a partnership, but – with DG Development marginalised, and impact assessments not widely available –

---

[6] Report on the Commission communication on an integrated framework for fisheries partnership agreements with third countries, 11 September 2003 – A5/0303/2003.

the process is currently much more of a commercial negotiation than a dialogue on sustainable development. Indeed, some developing countries remain to be convinced of the value of the new FPA approach, and would prefer to retain control over what is done with the financial compensation received rather than have to spend it on issues indicated by the EU. There is some discussion of fisheries issues at EU-ACP Joint Parliamentary Assembly, but little leverage over policy or particular negotiations.

An important innovation of the FPAs is the importance they place on scientific evidence of fisheries stocks, and of *ex ante* and *ex post* impact assessments. Impact assessments in this area do not have a good reputation, but if they are taken seriously and made available to all parties in a timely manner, they may provide a better basis for concluding sustainable fisheries agreements.

4. Lessons for policy coherence for development

The evolution of the integrated framework for FPAs with third countries and the negotiation of specific FPAs holds a number of lessons in terms of policy coherence for development:

- In an area of Commission competence, where DG Fisheries is in the lead, and where Council considerations are focused on fish rather than development, there is little formal opportunity for development inputs to be made in the Council's institutions. There may be value in institutional arrangements which require consultation with CODEV on an issue such as third-party fisheries agreements, which has important development implications.

- In the absence of effective entry points for development inputs within Council processes, coherence at member state level is especially important. Within member states, while policy coherence for development will only be attained once non-development ministries take account of development issues, development ministries will have to take the lead in making the case that fisheries policies have important development implications.

- Coherence at Commission level is equally crucial. DG Development ought to be involved in the design of any proposal, and the negotiation of any partnership, which has development implications. And the Development Cooperation Working Party should be kept informed by the Commission when partnership negotiations are planned.

- Reliable scientific data and timely, widely available impact assessments are essential to the formulation of policies which are coherent and supportive of development objectives. For policy proposals with development dimensions, independent assessments of the likely development impacts should be required.

- Delivering and implementing real policy coherence for development requires that developing countries are on board and that policies of partnership with the EU are an integral part of developing countries' strategies and plans. Attaining policy coherence for development in terms of EU policies is necessary but not sufficient.

- Policy coherence for development in bilateral relationships depends too on the activities of other countries. For instance, a fisheries agreement which appears sustainable would be rendered ineffective were the developing country to have entered into agreements with other fishing countries and failed to take this into account in its assessment of biological stocks.

7. Fiche on the Social Dimension of Globalisation, Employment and Decent Work

Michael Kaeding

1. Origins

According to the Treaty of Rome (1957), social policy competences were to remain largely a national affair. Yet in 1987, the Single European Act made one important exception: Art. 118a on minimum harmonisation concerning the health and safety of workers provided an escape route out of the unanimity requirement. For the first time in EU social policy, it allowed directives to be agreed on the basis of a qualified majority of the Council members. With the Treaty on European Union (TEU) (1992) signed in Maastricht, the Protocol on Social Policy (an additional, explicit social policy competence) was annexed to the EEC Treaty. This provision authorises member states to use the institutions, procedures (more majority voting) and mechanisms of the Treaty for the purpose of implementing the Social Chapter. The Amsterdam Treaty (1997) then transferred the innovations of the agreement on social policy to the main Treaty, making them binding for all. In addition, it introduced a new employment policy chapter providing for the coordination of national employment policies on the basis of annual guidelines and national follow-up reports.

Consequently, employment and social policy in the EU are subsumed under hard and soft law (the latter without binding legal constraints). The Commission has the right of initiative in the hard core legislative procedure covering the free movement of workers, labour, health and safety at work, gender equality and anti-discrimination. Whereas the important areas of employment and social protection have remained the exclusive responsibility of the member states, since the Amsterdam Treaty they have been coordinated through soft law, as it was acknowledged by the European Council that employment is a "matter of common concern" for the member states and one of the Community's goals (Falkner, 2003).

The Lisbon European Council of March 2000 asked member states and the European Commission to take steps to make a decisive impact on the eradication of poverty in the EU by 2010. More specifically, the Community's contribution consists of setting common objectives (social policy) or strategies (employment), analysing measures taken at the national level, monitoring progress towards the objectives and adopting recommendations to the member states (for employment). Here the EU strives to ensure that economic development is accompanied by social progress, not only within its own territory, but also internationally. It has therefore made social issues a subject of its external relations.

2. Main Council bodies involved

The Employment, Social Policy, Health and Consumer Affairs Council (EPSCO) is the most important Council of Ministers formation for decision-making on the social dimension of globalisation, employment and decent work. It meets about three times a year. The Economic and Finance Council (ECOFIN) and formations on competitiveness are sometimes involved or take decisions influencing the EU's policies in the field of employment and social affairs, mainly because of the Lisbon strategy.

At the level of working parties and the Committee of Permanent Representatives (Coreper), the matter is more complicated, mainly as a result of the division of competences between the Community and the EU member states. In the fields where the Commission has the right of initiative, there is the Working Party on Social Questions, which meets four times a month, depending on what is on the table in the form of Commission proposals. Coreper I usually deals with employment and social issues in the run up to each of the three annual Council meetings (March, June and December). It is very rare to submit files to Coreper for guidance outside of the context of preparation for a Council meeting, but it could be done and indeed does occur in other sectors (concerning the internal market, for example).

To coordinate the member states' policies there is the Employment Committee (EMCO) and the Social Protection Committee (SPC), which are independent advisory committees meeting outside the Council building. They monitor the development of national employment and labour market policies as well as social issues, and formulate opinions at the request of either the Council or Commission or on their own initiative. The SPC has established an Indicators Sub-Group to work on the development of indicators and statistics in support of its tasks. In any event, the EMCO and SPC conduct most of their work in the framework of the annual Lisbon cycle.

3. Applicable policy-making procedures

There are a great variety of decision-making procedures – varying from co-decision to consultation with the Council acting by qualified majority or unanimity and the open method of coordination (OMC). It is the issue at stake that determines which policy-making procedure is applied (Hervey, 1998).

The Council acts by qualified majority on matters such as determining the guidelines for member states to take into account in their employment policies (Art. 128(2)) and when it delivers recommendations to member states concerning employment policy (Art. 128(4)).

The Council acts by unanimity in areas defined by the Social Policy Protocol – social security and the social protection of workers, employment conditions for third-country nationals legally resident in Community territory and so forth. It also takes such action on measures necessary to combat all forms of discrimination based on gender, racial or ethnic origin, religion or belief, disability, age or sexual orientation (Art. 13).

Co-decision is used for the adoption of measures such as those on ensuring the application of the principle of equal opportunities and equal treatment of men and women in matters of employment and occupation (Art. 141(3)).

Finally yet importantly, the member states coordinate the European Employment Strategy (EES) and their policies for combating poverty and social exclusion and for reforming social protection systems on the basis of the *open method of coordination*. This method consists of the setting of common objectives, indicators and benchmarking, the exchange of best practices and monitoring at the EU level for social protection issues. This approach also involves setting up strategies for integrated guidelines on employment. The idea is that member states learn from each other's policies and are subject to peer review. Subsequently, they are free to choose how they want to achieve the common objectives/strategies and how they want to use the open method of coordination. Common strategies are adopted by the Council, acting by a qualified majority on a proposal from the Commission.

4. Principal parties involved in developing the policy: Background and level of seniority

In the hard core legislative procedure, the working party on employment and social questions receives the Commission's proposal. The working group normally consists of Brussels-based representatives of EU member states. Effectively, it is one working group with 'two teams'. National permanent representations to the EU send either their employment or social attachés to the meetings, which in fact makes it binary by nature. Then, the redrafted version of the proposal is sent directly to Coreper I and from there it is forwarded to the EPSCO.

In the soft law procedure, the EMCO and the SPC are responsible for preparing several issues dealt with by the Council, including the EES and its related instruments of employment guidelines, the joint employment report and the recommendations on the implementation of national employment policies and the social indicators in the context of the guidelines for social protection. Both the EMCO and the SPC consist of two representatives of each member state and the Commission. Normally, they represent higher levels of seniority compared with the working group, but the level of seniority has declined in recent years.

In the hard core legislative procedure as well as in the soft law sphere of social and employment policy, expert groups and comitology committees follow the policy-making cycle. There are 68 expert groups set up by the Commission to assist it in proposing EU legislation or exercising tasks of monitoring and coordination, consisting not only of national experts but also those representing stakeholders from business, NGOs, trade unions, academia, etc. In particular, there are 4 consultative and scientific groups, 25 permanent expert groups and 39 temporary groups. Examples here are the EQUAL Initiative and European Employment Services groups. Moreover, there are eight comitology committees on social and employment policy to assist the Commission in the implementation of EU legislation in the field, consisting of government representatives of the member states.[1]

---

[1] The comitology committees are: 1) the Committee on Employment Incentive Measures; 2) the Committee of the Community Action Programme to Encourage Cooperation between the Member States to Combat Social Exclusion; 3) the

5. Consultation and approval processes

Both the EMCO and the SPC work closely with other committees charged with working on EU social and economic policy, most notably the Economic Policy Committee.

In terms of the social dialogue, the Commission has to consult European employer and labour groups (social partners) before submitting proposals on a matter in order to reach a collective agreement. In terms of civil dialogue, the Commission consults with a network of NGOs and other bodies active in the social field. This network brings together around 1,000 representatives of NGOs and other bodies in a Forum on Social Policy.

In addition, expert groups provide independent advice to the Commission. Aside from offering a forum to exchange views, an expert group can advise the Commission throughout the policy process, from the policy development stage, through to decision-making and up to the implementation and evaluation phases. Comitology committees deliver opinions on draft implementing measures submitted to them by the Commission pursuant to the basic legislative instruments and intervene under the advisory, management or regulatory procedures provided for that purpose.

In the field of employment and social policy the European Parliament shares only limited legislative power with the Council. In some areas it is involved under consultation, whereas under the open method of coordination, Parliament plays no role at all. Other consultative bodies, such as the Economic and Social Committee (ECOSOC) are mainly concerned with labour policy, which gives it a particular perspective on more general social affairs. The Committee of Regions, established by the

---

Committee of the Community Action Programme to Combat Discrimination; 4) the Committee for the Technical Adaptation of Legislation on the Introduction of Measures to Encourage Improvements in the Safety and Health of Workers at Work; 5) the Committee for the Technical Adaptation of Legislation on the Minimum Safety and Health Requirements for Improved Medical Treatment on Board Vessels; 6) the Restricted Committee for Safety and Health in the Mining and other Extractive Industries; 7) the Disability Advisory Committee; and 8) the Committee for the Implementation of the Programme relating to the Community Framework Strategy on Gender Equality.

TEU, plays a role in the implementation of the EU's structural funds, especially the European Regional Development Fund.

6. Development policy input into the procedure

The EU has officially made social issues a subject of its external relations. It advocates compliance with core labour standards and promotes equal opportunities and non-discrimination beyond the borders of its member states, which it considers an integral part of human rights.

There are four core labour standards, identified at the Copenhagen World Summit for Social Development: freedom of association and real recognition of the right to collective bargaining; the elimination of all forms of forced or compulsory labour; the real abolition of child labour; and the elimination of discrimination in employment and occupation. The 1998 declaration by the International Labour Organisation (ILO) on fundamental principles and rights at work affirmed the universality of these core labour standards. Since 2002, the EU has agreed to monitor the work of the ILO's World Commission on the Social Dimension of Globalisation. On 19 July 2004 the Commission and the ILO even signed up to a strategic partnership to facilitate their operational cooperation in the developing countries. In fact, it is through the generalised system of preferences, for example, that the EU offers access to Community markets and additional trade preferences to those developing countries applying the core labour standards.

The EU also pursues its activities in equal opportunities and non-discrimination beyond the borders of its member states. For instance, the EU takes part in summits and conferences organised at the UN's initiative, for example on gender equality, the ageing of the world's population and social development. It contributes to the activities of the Economic and Social Council, the Commission for Social Development and the Commission on the Status of Women. Furthermore, the EU is in constant communication with the WTO and the OECD on employment and social policy issues. ·

7. Strengthening the process to secure a better development input

Since the EMCO and the SPC (the senior Council preparatory committees) conduct most of their work in the framework of the annual Lisbon cycle, development input could be provided at the expert-group level, the working-group level and/or Coreper. The history of the EMCO's role (Larsson, 2003) in EU employment policy illustrates the potential for strengthened coherence on development objectives. It has evolved from a small advisory committee to the Commission to a fully institutionalised, senior working committee within the Council framework. It is a good example of how an expert group can be used to influence the rest of the policy-making process by linking it to other institutions and arenas.

8. Organigram – Process and structures for the EU's social and employment policy in the EU Council

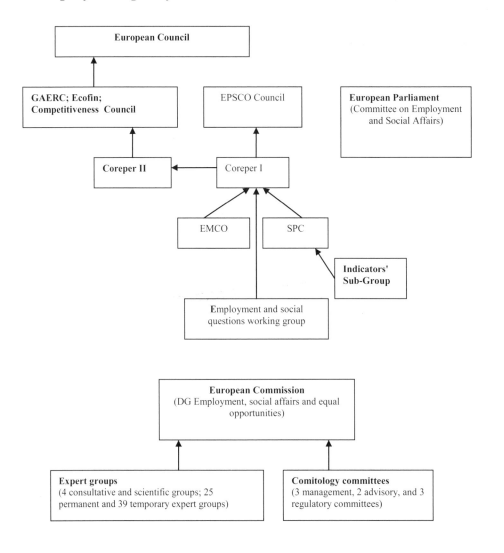

8. Fiche on EU Migration Policy

Sergio Carrera and Meng-Hsuan Chou

1. Origins

Immigration policies became a Community competence after the entry into force of the Amsterdam Treaty (1997).[1] The meeting of the European Council at Tampere in October 1999 represented a turning point in migration development: it was the first time a multi-annual programme was officially established. What came to be known as the Tampere Programme stressed that "the European Union needs a comprehensive approach to migration addressing political, human rights and development issues in countries and regions of origin and transit" (European Council, 1999). The European Commission then presented a Communication on a Community Immigration Policy (European Commission, 2000), which suggested closer cooperation with countries of origin to mitigate the effects of a brain drain and maximise the benefits of remittances.

The Commission Communication on a Policy Plan on Legal Migration (European Commission, 2005a) stressed "the need to enhance collaboration with third countries on economic migration and to develop initiatives offering 'win-win' opportunities to countries of origin and destination and to labour immigrants". The Commission envisages submitting a proposal by 2007 for a directive aimed at establishing a

---

[1] The Amsterdam Treaty transferred the Title IV provisions, which included "visas, asylum, immigration and other policies related to the free movement of persons", from the third pillar to the first. Yet it should be noted that in practice the parameters of these competences are still in the process of being defined. For example, although the Amsterdam Treaty has asked the Commission to propose legislation that would eventually lead to a common immigration policy, attempts by the Commission have been met with resistance by the member states, which has led to the withdrawal of several Commission proposals in this area. See, for example, European Commission, Proposal for a Council Directive on the conditions of entry and residence of third-country nationals for the purpose of paid employment and self-employed economic activities, COM(2001) 386 final, Brussels, 11.7.2001.

common framework of rights for all immigrants who are in legal employment and who have already been admitted to the EU territory. It will also elaborate four specific directives dealing with, respectively, highly skilled workers, seasonal workers, intra-corporate transferees and remunerated trainees.[2]

2. Main Council bodies involved

Two councils are involved in the making of migration policies, namely that on Justice and Home Affairs (JHA) and on General Affairs and External Relations (GAERC). The JHA Council, consisting of interior and justice representatives, has the primary responsibility of overseeing the policy-making process in relation to immigration. The GAERC only intervenes on issues that have an impact on external relations or contain an 'external dimension'. Immediately underneath the JHA Council is the Committee of Permanent Representatives (Coreper II), which as its name indicates consists of the permanent representatives of the EU member states, i.e. the top diplomats presiding over the permanent representations of their country to the EU. This juxtaposition of interior/justice and foreign representatives within a single, internal policy-making process of the Council is unique to migration matters. These permanent representatives meet weekly and prepare works for the interior/justice ministers.

Three committees falling immediately under Coreper II prepare JHA files, of which only the Strategic Committee on Immigration, Frontiers and Asylum (SCIFA) is specifically relevant to migration policies. SCIFA, also known as the 'Art. 66 Committee' of the Treaty establishing the European Community (TEC), consists of one interior ministry representative from each of the member states and one representative from the European Commission. It considers matters mainly relating to immigration, frontiers and asylum. Underpinning the SCIFA is a conglomerate of working parties. Issues concerning migration are mainly taken up by the Working Party on Migration and Expulsion, which covers topics related to both admission and expulsion of third-country nationals, and to a lesser extent the Visas Working Party and the Centre for Immigration, Discussion and Exchange

---

[2] The first two directives are expected to be presented between 2007 and 2008, and the last two by 2009.

on the Crossing of Frontiers and Immigration (CIREFI).[3] When EU migration policies contain an external dimension, the High-Level Working Group (HLWG) on Immigration and Asylum is called upon to draft the Council conclusions on the particular proposal. In policy development terms, the work of the HLWG is surely the most relevant.

3. Applicable policy-making procedures

The decision-making procedure for legal migration has remained the consultation process as outlined in Art. 67 of the TEC.[4] Under the terms of this process, the Council votes on a unanimity basis after consulting the opinion of the European Parliament. In practice, votes are never taken in the Council. Efforts are always made to garner consensus from all EU member states. Since May 2004, the Commission has had the exclusive right to initiate proposals.

4. Principal parties involved in developing the policy: Background and level of seniority

Once the Commission submits a proposal for a Council directive or regulation, it is considered by the competent working party. Members of working parties are technical experts seconded by EU member states. They are based at the member states' permanent representations. The agenda of the Council working party is mainly to discuss technical aspects of the

---

[3] The CIREFI is not a legislative working party; its role is purely that of information exchange. See European Council, List of Council Preparatory Bodies, 15180/05, Brussels, 5.12.2005(c).

[4] The use of the decision-making process outlined in Art. 67 TEC has been subject to criticism because of its perceived democratic deficit (see Balzacq, T. and S. Carrera, *Migration, Borders and Asylum: Trends and Vulnerabilities in EU Policy*, CEPS, Brussels, 2005). Since January 2005, the remaining areas of Title IV TEC have been transferred to the co-decision procedure, as stipulated in Art. 251 TEC. See European Council, Directive 2004/114/EC of 13 December 2004 on the conditions of admission of third-country nationals for the purposes of studies, pupil exchanges, unremunerated training or voluntary service, OJ L 375, 23.12.2004(b).

legislative proposals.[5] Political and strategic discussions generally do not take place at working party levels as these are done by the SCIFA. SCIFA members are senior officials, such as the heads of units, from the interior ministries.[6] If the SCIFA cannot find a consensus, these matters are passed on to Coreper II. When agreements are reached in either body, they become so-called 'A items'. Matters on which they have not managed to reach a consensus become 'B items', on which further discussion can take place in the JHA Council.

As previously mentioned, however, the HLWG deals with all migration issues containing an 'external dimension'. The HLWG mainly consists of representatives from the interior and justice ministries; they take political decisions and do not legislate.[7] Working parties that are traditionally within the JHA Council, such as the Working Party on Visas and Migration and Expulsion, can also be called upon to carry out preparatory work for the HLWG. Yet, as not all migration policies have an external dimension, these groups can be quite ad hoc. It is important to stress that the HLWG has and will continue to have a leading role on issues relating to migration that contain an external dimension such as migration policies dealing with development issues. Therefore, what we can observe in this cross-Council division in terms of competences on migration policies is the availability of venues allowing member states make their contributions on migration–development policies. The HLWG is not to be confused with the Committee on Immigration and Asylum (CIA), which is an expert group headed by the European Commission. CIA members are technical experts from and nominated by member states. Depending on the issue, usually one or two of these experts will be present during informal consultations in the proposal phase (comitology).[8]

---

[5] The working parties' agenda and minutes are immediately accessible on the Council's Register; however, this is not the case for LIMITE documents.

[6] For the Netherlands it is the Justice Ministry that deals with migration issues and in Spain it is the Social Affairs Ministry.

[7] For further discussion on the HLWG, see European Council, Modification of the terms of reference of the High-Level Working Group on Asylum and Migration (HLWG), 9433/02, Brussels, 30.5.2002(a).

[8] The CIA is an important component of the comitology process, as these experts are the liaisons between the Commission and the member states. For example, in

5. Consultation and approval processes

Formal and informal consultations occur throughout all stages of migration policy-making. Following this, it is also indicative that veto players abound. During the proposal phase, the Commission, relevant stakeholders, member states and national technical experts can all act as veto players on what subsequently reaches the EU immigration policy agenda. Moreover, it is perhaps during the adoption phase that one sees the most 'visible' veto actors, as there are strict procedural guidelines steering this process. Yet the 'invisible' veto factors include public opinion about migrants, public perceptions about the EU and national electoral pressures that might prevent member states from endorsing certain migration measures, even though some governments can see the potential benefits of a Community-wide migration policy.[9]

6. Development policy input into the procedure

Two approaches have emerged in EU member states on how to handle the nexus of migration and development, namely to: 1) use development tools to reach migration goals such as tackling illegal immigration; and 2) utilise migration tools such as legal immigration to achieve development objectives. The former represents a more 'coercive approach' in the form of restricting or conditioning development aid if certain non-EU countries do not comply with member states' requests on migration management and the readmission of illegal immigrants. The latter can be characterised as a more 'open approach', which seeks to foster the potential of 'brain circulation', circular migration and the positive effects of remittances.

---

the legislative process for deriving a common visa list, the Commission used the CIA extensively to sound out member states' positions with regard to the formulation of the questionnaire that was subsequently sent out to the member states.

[9] For an elaboration on the need to reconcile public concerns about immigration and Europe's demand for migrant labour, see Boswell, C., M.-H. Chou and J. Smith, *Reconciling Demand for Labour Migration with Public Concerns about Immigration: The cases of Germany and the UK*, Anglo-German Foundation, London (2005).

The coercive approach was very much championed by Spain and the UK during the Spanish presidency in 2002,10 but was ultimately abandoned at the EU level. Sweden and France, with the endorsement of Germany, pushed for migration diplomacy through co-development. Although efforts were made to resurrect the coercive approach in 2003, it was soundly rejected by the Greek presidency at the Council meeting in Thessaloniki.[11]

The Thessaloniki meeting was a watershed. Since then, although the establishment of an effective policy on illegal immigration remains a top priority for the EU, there seems to be a gradual move towards addressing development goals through legal migration instruments. This is particularly evident if we look at the 2005 Commission Communication on Migration and Development: Some Concrete Orientations (European Commission, 2005b).[12] In this Communication, the Commission explored the possibility, among other things, of having fast, secure and cheap ways of sending remittances, and the transfer of technology and skills through circular migration and brain circulation.[13]

---

[10] See European Council, Presidency Conclusions of the Seville European Council of 21-22 June, SN 13463/02, Brussels, 24.10.2002(b). In the same vein, see for example European Commission, Communication on Integrating Migration Issues in the European Union's Relations with Third Countries, COM(2002) 703 final, Brussels, 3.12.2002.

[11] See European Council, Presidency Conclusions of the Thessaloniki European Council of 19-20 June 2003, SN11638/03, Brussels, 1.10.2003(a). It is important to note that the Greek presidency expressly addressed the nexus between migration and development within the HLWG, which then led to the adoption of the Council Conclusions on this issue on 19 May 2003 (see European Council, Draft Council Conclusions on Migration and Development, 8927/03, Brussels (2003b).

[12] This Communication is part of The Hague Programme (see European Council, The Hague Programme: Strengthening Freedom, Security and Justice in the European Union, 2005/C53/01, OJ C 53/1, 3.3.2005(a)), which is the successor to Tampere.

[13] The most explicit proposal concerning development goals and migration is outlined in the European Commission's Communication on an EU Strategy for Action on the Crisis in Human Resources for Health in Developing Countries, COM(2005) 642 final, Brussels, 12.12.2005(f). But it should be noted that this

The 2005 British presidency welcomed the Commission's input on migration and development and asked the HLWG to draft a set of conclusions regarding migration and external relations (Council, 2005). These conclusions were adopted by the GAERC on 21 November 2005 (Council, 2005) with an eye towards the Commission Communication on a Policy Plan on Legal Migration (European Commission, 2005a). Here, the focus seems to have switched to a 'global approach' to migration, linking policy areas to the mobility of people – with priority actions focusing on the African and the Mediterranean regions, much of which follows a JHA agenda. In the GAERC conclusions, the Council also invited the Commission to analyse the recommendations made by the Global Commission on International Migration and to prepare EU's contribution to the UN's High-Level Dialogue on Migration and Development in September 2006.

Furthermore, the Council conclusions and programmes, as well as acts by the European Commission illustrate that inputs on development-related issues are introduced at every stage of the policy-making process. In this regard the contribution of the HLWG is more relevant than the input provided by the SCIFA. In the latter, political and strategic discussions concerning the external dimensions of migration policy take place. As noted earlier, the HLWG representatives are mainly interior and justice officials, but officials from the foreign ministries can also be present. For example, in the case of the UK, the delegations are comprised of representatives of the Foreign Office, Home Office and the Department for International Development; but it is the Home Office official who represents the UK in the HLWG.

Yet in spite of these external inputs, only the JHA Council can decide whether or not to translate them into EU legislation. It is clear that the Commission, given a mandate by the European Council, is adopting a 'lobbying' tactic, in which ideas are re-introduced in different guises throughout the evolution of cooperation on EU migration policy. The Commission believes that this strategy will permit non-JHA Council contributions to be incorporated into the law-making process. Thus far, only two pieces of legislation have addressed development issues through

---

Communication is an example of how development issues have taken migration matters into consideration, and not vice versa.

migration policies. These are: 1) the Council Directive (2004/114/EC) on the conditions of admission of third-country nationals for the purposes of studies, pupil exchanges, unremunerated training or voluntary services (Council, 2004); and 2) the Council Recommendation (2005/762/EC) on a specific procedure for admitting third-country nationals for the purposes of scientific research (Council, 2005). The Commission Communication on Migration and Development (European Commission, 2005) has expressly referred to these two instruments as playing a fundamental role in the development of skills, technology and capital within the framework of migration and development.

7. Strengthening the process to secure a better development input

Given the presence of the two dominant and diametrically-opposed strategies on addressing the nexus between migration and development, it is perhaps most important that the EU should resist using development tools to achieve migration goals. A continuing emphasis on reaching development objectives through legal migration tools will ensure that inputs to strengthen the process can continually be incorporated as the process evolves. Closely following this, if the EU is serious about reaching development objectives through migration tools, then EU legal instruments concerning circular migration, the protection of residence rights of migrant workers, and the facilitation of transfer of technology and skills to developing countries should also be adopted. As mentioned in the previous section, two legal instruments are already in place that utilise migration tools to achieve development objectives, and their exploitation and possible expansion within the development field should be encouraged. Along this vein, however, serious consideration should also be given to the financial and administrative burdens linked to the mobility of students and researchers, such as the issuing of visas and admissions fees for overseas students.

In policy development terms, the membership of the Council working groups can be supplemented if there was greater attendance by development Ministry representatives (if applicable) in the relevant working groups.

Furthermore, a simplification of the Council structure such as the elimination of the SCIFA, with regard to the existing venues in which member states can provide their contributions on migration-development issues, would also ensure that better development-related inputs will come to fruition. In the light of this, the structure could be simplified to the extent that inter-ministerial rivalries are not magnified at the EU level, which can often lead to policy stalemates on migration-related issues. If this can be achieved, one could more easily delineate where the responsibility lies and/or has been taken.

Although it might be true that transparency in the Council's activities has significantly improved since the Amsterdam Treaty, more progress is still needed – for example, in "the openness of the Council meetings when acting in its legislative capacity" (European Parliament, 2006). This would mean, in practice, that the entirety of the minutes should be made publicly accessible immediately.

Inclusiveness, simplification and transparency are in any case conditions for securing better contributions on the nexus between development and migration.

8. Organigram – Process and structures for the EU's migration policy in the EU Council

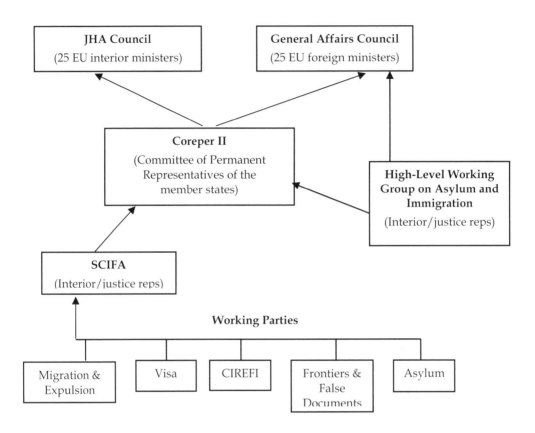

Case Study on EU Strategy for Action on the Crisis in Human Resources for Health in Developing Countries

Alan Hudson

The EU will strive to make migration a positive factor for development, through the promotion of concrete measures aimed at reinforcing the contribution to poverty reduction, including facilitating remittances and limiting the 'brain drain' of qualified people.[1]

1. Introduction

Identifying human resource constraints as a key barrier to the effective provision of health services in developing countries, in 2004 the 57th World Health Assembly – the governing body of the World Health Organisation – designated 2006-15 as a decade of action on human resources. The EU strategy for action on the crisis in human resources for health in developing countries outlines the response of the EU and the European Commission in particular to the WHO's decade of action.

The EU's strategy builds on the Commission's May 2005 Communication on A European Programme for Action to Confront HIV/AIDS, Malaria and Tuberculosis through External Action.[2] In that Communication, the lack of health workers was identified as a major obstacle to effective action. The EU's strategy also builds on that it outlined for Africa.[3] The strategy for action was adopted by the General Affairs and External Relations Council (GAERC) on 10 April 2006.

---

[1] See para. 38 of the European Consensus on Development, OJ C 46/01, 24.02.2006.

[2] See European Commission, Communication on a European Programme for Action to Confront HIV/AIDS, Malaria and Tuberculosis through External Action, COM(2005) 179 final, Brussels, 27.4.2005(c).

[3] See European Commission, Communication on an EU Strategy for Africa: Towards a Euro-African Pact to Accelerate Africa's Development, COM(2005) 489 final, Brussels, 12.10.2005(e).

2. Implications for development

The crisis in human resources for health in developing countries is of great importance to these countries and regions across the world. Africa, for instance, has the highest disease burden of any continent, but the lowest number of health workers. Africa has 0.8 health workers per 1,000 population, compared with 10.3 per 1,000 in Europe. There are many reasons why developing countries lack the human resources (health workers) they need to provide effective and adequate health services. These include poor working conditions as a result of years of under-investment, a lack of training, demoralisation, low salaries and other inadequate incentives.

One fundamental reason for the lack of human resources is that many health workers in developing countries, and particularly in rural areas of developing countries, opt to migrate to either urban areas, neighbouring countries, or internationally to Europe or North America. As such, the crisis in human resources for health in developing countries has a critical migration dimension. For the crisis to be addressed instrumentally, greater coherence is needed between the migration and development policies of the EU and other developed countries.

The EU's strategy for action includes a range of measures to support developing countries to address the crisis in human resources for health. These include the provision of support at a country level, at a regional level (through the African Union and the New Partnership for Africa's Development in the case of Africa) and at the global level. At the global level, the strategy commits the EU to exploring the value and feasibility of a code of conduct for ethical recruitment. This is the element of the strategy for action that raises policy coherence challenges. Put differently, there is little point in the EU spending development funds in building the capacity of developing countries' health systems, if the health workers needed to deliver services then migrate to the EU and beyond. A code of conduct for ethical recruitment would seek to ensure greater policy coherence for development.

3. EU (Council) players, processes and development inputs

The European Commission was responsible for initiating the strategy for action. The Directorate General (DG) for Development took the lead and informally consulted colleagues in the Europe Aid Coordination Office

(AIDCO), the DG for External Relations (RELEX), and the DG for Health and Consumer Protection (SANCO) on an early draft of the Communication, as part of the process of preparing the Communication on Action to Confront HIV/AIDS, Malaria and Tuberculosis (European Commission, 2005c). Beyond the Commission, the DG for Development consulted extensively with member states prior to launching the Communication for formal inter-service dialogue. At that stage, a number of DGs provided formal feedback, including AIDCO, DG RELEX, the DG for Employment, the DG for Information Society and Media, the DG for Justice, Freedom and Security, the DG for Research, and DG SANCO, who were concerned to ensure cross-reference to DG SANCO's work on internal EU health policies.

As regards coherence with the EU's approach to migration, it is important to note that the planned Communication was in line with the Commission's Communication on Migration and Development, published in September 2005.[4] That Communication, the production of which had been led by DG Justice, Freedom and Security, included sections on mitigating the adverse effect of brain drain, mentioning the possibility of an EU code of conduct to discipline recruitment. Yet in preparing the Communication on the human resources crisis in health, the Commission was keen to emphasise that the migration and brain drain of health workers, while an important cause of the human resource crisis, is not the only cause.

Beyond the Commission, there was much consultation with member states' technical experts on health issues. An important focus for these consultations was the member states' health expert forum. This informal group is attended by a representative from each member state, and can play an important role in providing guidance to the Commission. After these discussions, which served to clarify several issues and to put the matter on member states' agendas, member states/the Council invited the Commission to prepare a communication on the crisis in human resources for health in developing countries. The UK – holding the presidency in late 2005 – was particularly active in pushing for a code of recruitment for health service personnel, having established its own guidelines some years

---

[4] See European Commission, Communication on Migration and Development: Some Concrete Orientations, COM(2005) 390 final, Brussels, 1.9.2005(b).

earlier. Consultations also took place with developing countries, including through the Secretariat for African, Caribbean and Pacific (ACP) countries. The Commission produced its Communication to the Council and the European Parliament in December 2005.[5]

The Council's Working Party on Development Cooperation (CODEV) was the key player in examining the Commission's proposal. After several meetings and much informal dialogue between the Commission and the CODEV, the latter agreed to a set of draft conclusions that it had invited Coreper to submit to the GAERC for adoption. GAERC adopted the conclusions on 10 April 2006, only four months after the initial Commission Communication.[6] Despite the fact that the EU action plan puts progress on disciplining ethical recruitment – an issue that is at the interface of migration and development – at the top of its list of priority actions, there is no evidence of CODEV consultation with the High-Level Working Group on Asylum and Immigration, the key Council institution for migration issues.

4. Lessons for policy coherence for development

Although this case study is about efforts to achieve coherence between development and other policies in a development context, it nevertheless holds some useful lessons for policy coherence for development in general:

- Efforts to attain policy coherence for development involve not only pushing development objectives in non-development arenas, but also ensuring that objectives for development and other issues are dealt with coherently in fora on development. CODEV and the development community should seek to include other interests in their discussions, at the same time as seeking to inject development concerns into non-development arenas.

---

[5] See European Commission, Communication on an EU Strategy for Action on the Crisis in Human Resources for Health in Developing Countries, COM(2005) 642 final, Brussels, 12.12.2005(f).

[6] See European Council, Conclusions from the General Affairs and External Relations Council meeting on an EU strategy for action on the crisis in human resources for health in developing countries, Luxembourg, 10.4.2006(a).

- Consultation between the Commission and member states prior to the formal Commission inter-service consultation seems to have been very useful in helping to ensure that the various DGs understood the member states' wishes. This dialogue between the member states and the Commission smoothed the process of inter-service consultation.

- While there seems to have been excellent communication between the Commission and member states, and among the various DGs, there seems to have been little communication between the migration and development streams of Council, either at the level of working parties or the Council itself. Consultation among the different Council streams should be required when issues that spill over institutional boundaries are being discussed.

- External champions – in this case the ACP countries – can play an important role in stimulating and supporting EU policy initiatives. Indeed, on issues where there are major development implications, the input of developing countries should be actively sought.

Finally, member states with prior experience of implementing initiatives intended to achieve greater policy coherence for development can play an important role in encouraging the EU as a whole to adopt similar measures.

9. Fiche on EU Research Policy

Louise van Schaik

1. Origins

European research policy originated in the Coal and Steel Community (1950) and later in the context of the EURATOM Treaty (1957), which includes a multi-annual EURATOM research Framework Programme (Art. 7) and the Joint Research Centre, whose mandate has since been enlarged to include a large non-nuclear work programme as well. Within the scope of the EC Treaty, research policy was gradually developed through sectoral initiatives such as ESPRIT (on information technologies) or BRITE/EURAM (on industrial and materials technologies), under the strategic supervision of the high-level advisory committee CREST (*Comité de recherche scientifique et technique*).

Since 1986, European Community research policy has been managed through the multi-annual Framework Programmes (FPs) for Research and Development. While earlier FPs had a duration period of five years, the proposed FP7 will extend to seven years, in parallel with the Financial Perspectives (2007-13). Currently FP6 is in place, which runs for the period 2002-06 with a budget of €17.5 billion. Under this programme, research is undertaken in seven thematic priority areas.

At the time of writing, negotiations on FP7 are in full swing after the Commission adopted the FP7 proposal on 6 April 2005.[1] The proposal contains four specific programmes: cooperation (which includes several thematic priorities), ideas, people and capacities, each of which contains resources for international activities. The programme is to run from 2007 to 2013. The Commission has proposed a budget of €64.5 billion, which has been reduced to €50.2 billion in the context of the agreement set on the EU's overall budgetary framework. This figure will amount to a 60% increase in

---

[1] The European Commission's key documents and proposals for the programmes of FP7, as well as the rules for participation and so forth can be downloaded from the Commission's Research website (http://europa.eu.int/comm/research/future/documents_en.cfm#communication).

resources in comparison with FP6, reflecting the EU's increased attention on research as a strategic aspect of stimulating economic growth. An added novelty is the proposed European Research Council, a body that is to allocate a considerable portion of the resources of FP7 to investigator-driven 'frontier' research on the basis of academic excellence through an open competition.

Research already comes third in terms of EU spending, just after agriculture and regional development. One of the goals of EU research policy is better policy coordination, as research policy is still an area in which the Community only has a complementary competence.[2] Indeed, most of the spending for research is still allocated at the national level[3] and a recurring argument is not only that research spending is generally lower in the EU than in the US and Japan, but more dispersed and fragmented as well, leading to lesser output per euro spent. This situation can be particularly problematic given the strategic importance of R&D for maintaining a competitive position *vis-à-vis* the rest of the world, as is the key objective of the Lisbon strategy. The budget is a sensitive issue for the EU member states, although they generally tend to be protective when it comes to sharing authority over resources for spending on public research. Further, they carefully check the distributive effects of the FPs and particularly look after their own shares (Banchoff, 2002).

To redirect the focus from the concrete projects in the FPs to research policy for the EU overall, the concept of a European Research Area (ERA) has been launched in conjunction with FP6. Its aim is the creation of a genuine 'internal market' in research to increase pan-European cooperation and coordination of national research activities by 2010. Currently, the triangular relationship between education, research and innovation is becoming a dominant theme for thinking about EU research policy.

---

[2] Ratification of the Constitutional Treaty would see research become a shared competence.

[3] According to Banchoff (2002), member states still account for around 95% of public civil research and development expenditures in the EU.

2. Main Council bodies involved

Legislative proposals on research policy are negotiated in the Working Party on Research, which normally meets about once or twice a week, but with different topics on the agenda. Now, with decision-making on FP7 moving towards its final stages, the group meets more often. When needed, further discussions and negotiations take place in the Committee of Permanent Representatives (Coreper I), and subsequently in the competitiveness formation of the Council of Ministers.

Member states' policies are coordinated by CREST, the EU's scientific and technical research advisory body, which is composed of member states' representatives. Its function is to assist the Council and the Commission in performing the tasks incumbent on them in the sphere of research and technology development (RTD). CREST meets about four to six times a year and supervises five expert groups along with a steering group on human resources and mobility. The focus of the latter group is probably the most important from a development perspective as it covers the position of researchers from non-EU countries (including developing countries). The expert groups gather about once a month and monitor aspects of the research policies of the EU member states through comparing statistics, benchmarking policies, peer review, identifying best practices, etc. On the basis of this analysis CREST formulates opinions at the request of either the Council or Commission or on its own initiative. CREST conducts its work in the context of the Lisbon process and is one of the bodies applying the open method of coordination (OMC) (see below).

3. Applicable policy-making procedures

The final decision on FP7 will be taken through the co-decision procedure on the basis of Art. 166. The rules of participation in undertakings, research centres and universities along with the rules governing the dissemination of research results are also decided upon by co-decision (Art. 167). Although the European Parliament is involved as co-legislator on FP7, this is only with regard to the overall framework and principles governing the programme. The specific programmes, in line with Arts. 166§3 and 166§4 are decided upon by the Council through the consultation procedure. In practice, however, the European Parliament can threaten to withhold its approval on the FP unless more information on the specific programmes is revealed.

The open method of coordination, which is used to coordinate the national research policies of the EU member states, is a soft law approach not enshrined in the EC Treaty. It consists of the setting of common objectives, indicators and benchmarking, the exchange of best practices and monitoring at the EU level. The idea is that member states learn from each other's policies and are subject to peer review. Subsequently, they are free to choose how they want to achieve the common objectives/strategies and how they want to use the OMC. Strategies are adopted by the Council, acting by a qualified majority on a proposal from the Commission.

4. Principal parties involved in developing the policy: Background and level of seniority

Within the European Commission, the Directorate General (DG) for Research is in the lead when it comes to legislative proposals on research. Yet on some topics (e.g. energy, transport and information society) other DGs such as those on Energy and Transport, Information Society and Media, Enterprise, Fisheries, Health and Consumer Protection (SANCO), Agriculture and Environment have a keen interest in following and influencing EU priorities for research.

Moreover, the Commission has a strong role in the implementation of the FPs: it drafts and publishes the calls for research, moderates committees of scientific experts that evaluate the proposals, conducts the contract negotiations and finally transfers the funds that pay for the research project. The final approval on calls for research, the work programmes accompanying them, the evaluation criteria and ultimately the decision on the selection of research projects is the task of so-called 'programme committees' established by the specific programmes of the FP. These are chaired by the Commission and composed of member states' representatives. They follow the general rules of the Council's comitology Decision (Council Decision 468/1999/EC of 28 June 1999). For the selection of projects they draw heavily on the ranking made by the evaluation committees of scientific experts.

In FP7 the Commission proposes to have all logistical and administrative tasks – i.e. those not related to policy – undertaken outside its services by executive agencies, in order to be able to manage the sharply increased resources in a more efficient way. The Commission would thus be less concerned with the implementation of the FP and more with the development of research policies for the ERA.

As previously noted, a new body is envisaged to take over tasks from the European Commission on an increasing basis, the European Research Council, which would be charged with directing some of the research budget towards projects they consider to be of academic excellence. Under FP7 larger portions of the budget will be allocated through the European Research Council – around one-sixth of the total budget for FP7, if the Commission's proposal is followed.

In the European Parliament, research is the prerogative of the Industry, Research and Energy (ITRE) Committee, with other committees closely following the file and sometimes indirectly influencing it, notably the Budget Committee when looking at the EU's financing.

The participants of the Council Working Party on Research are attachés from the permanent representations, sometimes seconded by national experts from the capitals. CREST and its expert groups are staffed by policy-makers from the national ministries, with CREST being staffed by very senior officials and the expert groups by somewhat less senior representatives. The programme committees are staffed mainly by national officials, who normally supervise and carry out the implementation of national research programmes.

5. Consultation and approval processes

Coordination of national research policies is a sensitive issue as it involves relatively large budgets and is sometimes closely related to the strategic choices of states (e.g. to invest more in renewable energy research versus nuclear options or in the health sector). When it comes to research coordination, for a long time member states have seemed to favour intergovernmental solutions over delegating activities to the Commission. For instance, in the mid-1990s the member states strengthened CREST and the individual programme committees looking after FP formulation and implementation. They also established EUREKA, an intergovernmental technology project on defence matters (Banchoff, 2002).

Yet the framing of research policy in the context of the Lisbon process has changed the focus of the member states to a certain extent. This change is most evident in the creation of the European Research Council, where the programme committee is likely to be involved only with regard to ethical research questions (e.g. stem cell research).[4] It is also obvious in the decision of member states to make research an area of shared competence under the Constitutional Treaty, the ratification of which, however, is currently blocked by the negative outcome of the French and Dutch referenda.

Concerning the priorities set in the FPs, the Commission consults widely on its proposals with relevant stakeholders in the research community.

6. Development policy input into the procedure

In 1994 the Commission first proposed to include strategic programmes for international cooperation in the EU's research policy. Attention to broader policy questions was given in the Communication on the International Dimension of the European Research Area (European Commission, 2001b). For the life of FP6, a budget of €658 million has been available for international scientific cooperation (INCO) activities involving non-EU countries or regions. The aim is to support projects that bolster the EU's external relations and development aid policies – particularly as they relate to the fight against poverty, the Community's water initiatives and its commitment to the UN's Millennium Development Goals. There are also some sums available for international research mobility. The Commission is currently drafting a new communication on INCO activities that is due to be published in summer 2006.

In addition, under FP6 there is one specific project, the European and Developing Countries Clinical Trials Partnership (EDCTP),[5] in which the Community participates in a research project involving developing countries along with several member states plus Norway. The EU finances €200 million, about one-third of the total budget. The objective is to translate medical research results on certain diseases that particularly afflict the developing world – including HIV/AIDS, malaria and tuberculosis –

---

[4] Although this aspect of FP7 is still subject to ongoing negotiations, it is likely that the European Research Council only has to refer to the programme committee when ethical questions arise in the call for research.

[5] For further information on the project, see the European Commission's Research website (http://ec.europa.eu/comm/research/info/conferences/edctp).

into clinical applications tailored to the developing countries. The clinical trials are conducted in sub-Saharan African countries that participate in the project. The project is the first in which Art. 169 (TEC) is used, allowing the participation of the Community in member states' joint national research and development programmes. The EDCTP owes its creation very much to a determined effort by the Commission, rather than being a bottom-up initiative from the member states. Community participation was decided upon by the Competitiveness Council by co-decision with strong backing by the European Parliament.

In terms of policy, further interest in the relationship between research and development was sparked in 2004 by an EU presidency conference on brain drain – the loss of the skills and knowledge of well-trained people who migrate to the Western world[6] (see also the migration case study in this report). The conference concluded that sub-Saharan Africa would be particularly vulnerable to brain drain to the Western world and argued for a targeted cooperation programme. A preparatory expert meeting[7] emphasised that Europe is quite often used by researchers as a transit location to gain knowledge and experience needed in order to move on to more attractive regions, meaning the US and Canada. In that respect the EU should focus on either keeping the researchers in which it has invested, or – and perhaps more importantly – on creating favourable conditions for undertaking research efforts in the home country.

Under FP7 the Commission has proposed that international cooperation in FP7 will no longer be a separate part of the programme, but will be integrated in all four programmes, allowing projects to be carried out with international partners. There is a fear that the negotiations on the budget and the strong focus on the EU's competitive position *vis-à-vis* the

---

[6] The conclusions and recommendations of the EU conference "Brain Gain – The Instruments" held in The Hague on 29-30 September 2004 are available on the website for the Netherlands Organisation for International Cooperation in Higher Education (Nuffic) (http://www.nuffic.net/common.asp?id=1013).

[7] See the Netherlands Organisation for International Cooperation in Higher Education (Nuffic), *Report of the expert meeting on migration, brain drain and development*, from the meeting held on 11 December 2003 in Scheveningen, Nuffic, The Hague (2003).

rest of the world will detract attention from the problematic issues of brain drain and research capacity-building, particularly in Africa.

Apart from the FPs, some of the budget of the European Development Fund is allocated to R&D activities in developing countries and there are some bilateral agreements with developing countries that have an R&D component (e.g. the partnerships on clean energy and climate with India and China). In 2001 the total expenditure allocated by the 18 EU and European Economic Area countries to bilateral RTD cooperation with all non-EU countries was estimated at around €750 million annually. Some 20% of this would be allocated to international cooperation programmes with developing countries. Another 25% would be sent to Africa to develop RTD activities and improve research capability (European Commission, 2001b).

7. Strengthening the process to secure a better development input

As with all Commission proposals, FP7 and its specific programmes have gone through inter-service consultation within the Commission before being adopted by the College of Commissioners. But the proposal gives little attention to specific activities to stimulate research in developing countries, making it more difficult for the Council to reinforce this aspect. Moreover, to date it lacks any concrete suggestion for further projects under Art. 169 (like the EDCTP, but in other fields such as agriculture, energy and biodiversity).

A way of focusing attention on the issue of research in relation to the economic development of the least-developed countries would be for the Commission to issue a specific communication on research policy in the context of development cooperation, something that development experts in EU member states and the participants of Council's Working Party on Development Cooperation (CODEV) could argue for on the basis of the inclusion of research in the Council conclusions on policy development.

Another option to strengthen the development input in research policy-making could be to ask CREST to take up the issue of policy coherence for development in their benchmark activities for spending on national research programmes, either directly or through their expert groups.

Finally, the issue of brain drain is very much one for the domain of justice and home affairs, as is illustrated by the case study on migration later in this report. Development experts could give a stronger emphasis to the particular importance of brain drain in sub-Saharan Africa and see how this issue could garner more attention in policy-making on migration (e.g. the ethical guidelines used for health workers could also be applied to academic researchers).

In general, it seems to be the case that the research–development interface is greatly influenced by the Councils on Justice and Home Affairs and Competitiveness. With their main focus respectively on limiting migration to the EU and the economic position of the EU *vis-à-vis* the rest of the world, it may not be realistic to expect that they would automatically see the link with development goals or fully understand it. In that respect, awareness-raising, for instance through the drafting of a communication on the topic or through a follow-up conference organised by the presidency, could be an effort worth pursuing.

Finally, the CODEV and the General Affairs and External Relations Council could argue that, when making their decisions about FP7, more explicit mention should be made of those parts of the budget that will be allocated to non-EU countries, and in particular what share will go to increasing the research capacities of the least-developed countries.

8. Organigram – Process and structures for the EU's research policy with a focus on the EU Council

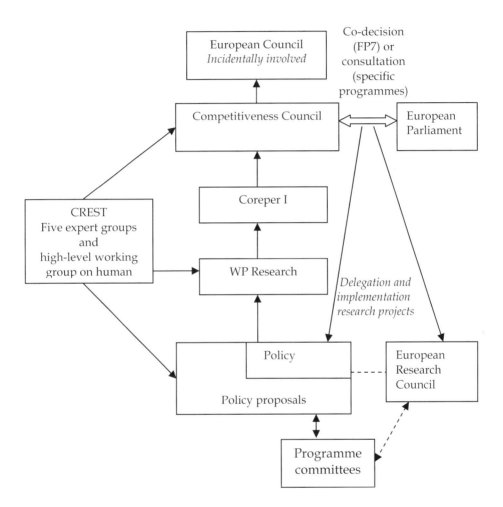

10. Fiche on EU Information Society Policy

Lorna Schrefler

1. Origins

Information society is a relatively new arrival in European policy-making. Since the beginning, the policy has been based on two main pillars, R&D in information and communications technologies (ICT) and telecommunications policy, whose foundations can be traced back respectively to the mid-1980s with the ESPRIT Programme on R&D activities in ICT and the 1987 Green Paper on telecommunications liberalisation.[1] The 1994 Commission's Communication on the information society[2] constitutes a further step in devising the EU's approach and strategy in this policy area.

Policy on the information society is encompassing in nature and thus affects many areas of Community intervention, including the competitiveness of the internal market, competition, enterprise, education, content and media, and development policies. Moreover, technological convergence and the increasing importance of information as an economic resource make it a pivotal tool to promote growth and competitiveness in the so-called 'knowledge-based economy' described by the Lisbon strategy. For these reasons, EU institutions have adopted a proactive approach, urged on by the fact that other countries are investing in the information society and Europe cannot afford to lag behind.[3]

---

[1] See European Commission, *Towards a Dynamic European Economy, Green Paper on the Development of the Common Market for Telecommunications Services and Equipment*, COM(87) 290, Brussels, June 1987.

[2] See the European Commission's Communication on Europe's Way to the Information Society – An Action Plan, COM(94) 347 final, Brussels, 10.7.1994.

[3] For further details, see European Council, *Recommendations to the European Council – Europe and the Global Information Society*, Report prepared by the High-Level Group on the Information Society ('Bangemann Report'), 26 May 1994; see also European Commission, Communication on Challenges for the European Information Society beyond 2005, COM(2004) 757 final, Brussels, 19.11.2004 and

2. Main Council bodies involved

Despite its pervasive nature, information society policy is dealt with mainly through a traditional three-level approach: working parties, the Committee of Permanent Representatives (Coreper I) and the Council of Ministers. There are two Council configurations responsible for the dossier, depending on the policy aspect at stake. The Council for Transport, Telecommunications and Energy, meeting under the Council of Telecommunications Ministers, deals with matters related to electronic communications. The Competitiveness Council is in charge of other areas of information society policy such as research, e-commerce and internal market issues.

Preparations are generally conducted by the Working Party on Telecommunications and Information Society (H.5), whose experts meet around 24 times a year. Other working parties can potentially influence the decision-making process, namely on issues related to internal market harmonisation or to crucial areas for the Lisbon strategy, which fall into the domain of the Competitiveness Council. In particular, the Working Parties on Competitiveness and Growth (G.1), Technical Harmonisation (G.7), Competition (G.13) and Research (G.14) provide relevant input and direction to form the policy early on in its technical aspects. Joint meetings between these working parties and the Telecommunications and Information Society Working Party happen very rarely, thus their respective dossiers tend to remain separate.

Subsequently, work continues in Coreper I and finally at the ministerial level. The Council of Telecommunications Ministers meets approximately three times per year, while Competitiveness Council meetings are normally held every two or three months.

3. Applicable policy-making procedures

Even if not specifically outlined by the EC Treaty, information society policy influences many areas of Community intervention and is thus grounded in various provisions regarding competition (Arts. 81 to 89),

---

European Commission, Communication on i2010 – A European Information Society for Growth and Employment, COM(2005) 229 final, Brussels, 31.5.2005(g).

internal market harmonisation (Art. 95), and to a lesser extent the right of establishment and services (Arts. 47 and 55). Moreover, the legal basis for the support of research and development in ICT technology lies in Arts. 163-173, while the impact on the competitiveness of Community industry is governed by Art. 157. Finally, Arts. 154-156 TEC establish the promotion of trans-European networks (TENs) for transport, energy and telecommunications.

The broad scope of the policy is reflected in the distribution of Community competences for policy-making, which can be exclusive or mixed, depending on the characteristics of the particular case at hand. For instance, with regard to external policy, when Community intervention is linked to the common commercial policy, the EU has exclusive competence on the basis of Art. 133 TEC. This is also the case for all bilateral agreements between the EU and non-EU countries, governing the commercial aspects of the information society policy.[4] For all other areas of external policy, for example the cooperation in international programmes coordinated by inter-governmental agencies, the EU has mixed competence together with the member states.

Legislative acts are generally adopted following the co-decision procedure (Art. 251). The right of initiative belongs to the Commission. In many cases, the Economic and Social Committee has to be consulted. The Council usually votes by qualified majority. Unanimity-based voting can be necessary when the Council's position differs from that of the Commission or the European Parliament. Political files are adopted by consensus as conclusions or resolutions, which have no legally binding power.

4. Principal parties involved in developing the policy: Background and level of seniority

The contributions to policy development at the EU level come from the European Commission, through the DG Information Society and Media. Some of the initial ingredients of the policy proposal can also be based on

---

[4] See, for example European Council, Decision 2003/840/EC of 17 November 2003 relating to the conclusion on behalf of the European Community of Council of Europe Convention No. 180 on information and legal cooperation on information society services, OJ L 321, 06.12.2003(c), pp. 41-42.

input by the member states (i.e. on the initiative of a certain number of member states within the Council itself, on the experience or the suggestions of national regulatory authorities) or can stem from the advisory role of the European Regulators Group (ERG), the Independent Regulators Group (IRG) and ad hoc committees.[5] These bodies are composed of representatives of the member states, members of the Commission and, when relevant, the heads of the competent national authorities and play an important role throughout the whole policy process. For example, some of them are involved in comitology when specific requirements, such as prices or market conditions, are imposed by a directive/legislative act and need to be modified for the information society policy to work.

Other inputs for policy development can originate from broader consultations with relevant trade associations such as ETNO, ECTA, ECCA, INTUG and the GSM Association.[6]

In a secondary stage, the Commission's proposal is submitted to the appropriate working party in the Council for technical and policy aspects to be tackled by national experts, normally Brussels-based diplomats, before being passed to Coreper I. Finally, the dossier moves on to the Telecommunications or Competitiveness Council. The majority of issues (around 90%) are solved at the working party level. When the subject at stake is among of the priorities of the presidency, the latter plays a relevant role in accelerating the policy-making procedure, through agenda-setting mechanisms and by reconciling positions in the drafts that are usually supplied before the Council itself meets.

---

[5] For instance, on the basis of the new regulatory framework for electronic communications, several committees have been created to assist the European Commission in its work on the e-communications aspects of information society policy, namely the Communications Committee, the Radio Spectrum Committee, the Radio Spectrum Policy Group and the Working Party on the Protection of Individuals with regard to the Processing of Personal Data, known as the 'Art. 29 Working Party'.

[6] For the full names of these associations, see the Glossary of Abbreviations and Terms in this report.

5. Consultation and approval processes

As the co-decision procedure is generally applied for information society policy, the role of the European Parliament is gaining ground. Moreover, owing to the multifaceted aspect of the policy itself, there are various levels of intervention. Three parliamentary committees with different portfolios have competence on the information society dossier. The Committee on Industry, Research and Energy deals with the industrial policy implications of the information society agenda and more specifically with information society and information technology aspects affecting the development of TENs in the telecommunications infrastructure. The Committee on Civil Liberties, Justice and Home Affairs addresses all possible effects of information technologies on citizen's rights, such as the protection of privacy, the processing of personal data and so on. Finally, the Committee on Culture and Education acts on information and media policy and on the international aspects of cooperation in education and culture. For every legislative act, the rapporteur is a key player in the interaction between the European Parliament and the Council and has considerable influence on the final outcome of the co-decision procedure.

Advisory bodies such as the ERG, the high-level groups[7] and other specific fora set up by the European Commission provide it with political guidance and advice on drafting the legislative proposal. As previously mentioned, the latter are also involved in further stages of the process, to facilitate a correct and harmonised implementation of the policy. The consultative role of the Economic and Social Committee (ECOSOC), embedded in the co-decision procedure itself, also shapes the consultation processes of policy-making.

6. Development policy input into the procedure

Development goals are only indirectly linked to information society agenda and are not a core priority in the dossiers. Nevertheless, the EU is well aware of the international dimension of its policy and of its potential for the achievement of the UN Millennium Development Goals. This was clearly

---

[7] Among these are the High-Level Expert Group on the i2010 Strategy and the High-Level Group on Internet Governance (HLIG).

stated during the World Summit on the Information Society (WSIS) in Tunis in November 2005. More generally, ICTs are considered an appropriate tool to promote and facilitate education and good governance. As with other aspects of the policy, inputs come from the Commission, but owing to the political dimension, mixed competences and the international visibility of development objectives, the roles of the Council and the member states in these international fora are key. For example, in the case of the WSIS, the EU position was drafted by the European Commission together with the presidency. During the summit, the presidency spoke on behalf on the EU in order to have a single and thus more powerful voice in the context of a UN event, where EU member states were also individually represented.

7. Strengthening the process to secure a better development input

It is important to note that the amount of funding allocated for information society issues within development policy is generally not clearly identifiable, as it is incorporated in the total financial aid directed to a specific country. It is normally the government of the targeted country that chooses the amount of resources to apply to information society initiatives, thus rendering sectoral policy orientations more difficult to influence. Only in some cases is targeted funding easily recognisable, as interventions are linked to specific programmes such as @LIS or EUMEDIS. The distance between the different areas of policy intervention is increased by the fact that decisions on development aspects, including those concerning information society issues, are taken in the framework of the General Affairs and External Relations Council, without direct input from the specialised working parties normally dealing with the technical and internal aspects of the policy. This might lead to a dispersion of precious contributions and thus to less coherent policy-making.

Given the greater political context associated with development issues when compared with the rather technical character of information society matters, the policy process could be strengthened by increasing internal coordination and cooperation within the Council. As previously stated, the majority of issues are discussed and solved at the working party level. Thus, the creation of joint task forces among the relevant working parties could secure a coherent inclusion of development inputs in the various aspects of the information-society policy process.[8] To maximise the impact of increased internal coordination, the structure of the General Secretariat could be rearranged to ensure that all actors dealing with such a broad policy are informed of activities on different fronts of Community intervention and can provide a valuable contribution. This step would stimulate a change in the administrative culture and develop an internal awareness of development problems in a field that is partly isolated from the topic.

Such an approach could be fostered now by including development inputs in the *ex-ante* impact assessments carried out by the Commission, where relevant. In that respect, lessons learned at the institutional level in sectors that have a greater track record of dealing with development aspects of Community policies could be translated to the information society field. This move would create a sort of 'institutional convergence' that strongly mirrors one of the intrinsic and most challenging technical characteristics of the information society policy itself.

---

[8] This suggestion is reflected by the dotted red-line in the *organigramme* in section 8.

8. Organigram – Process and structures for the EU's information society policy

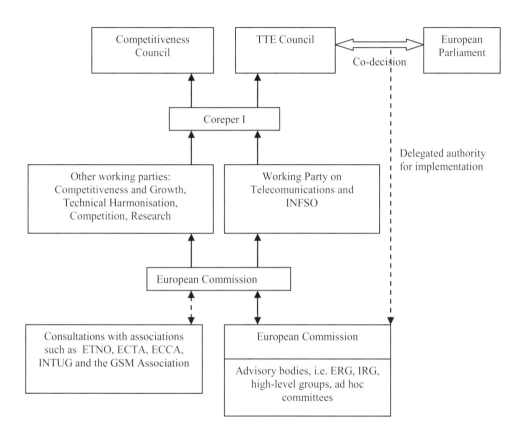

11. Fiche on EU Transport Policy

Michael Kaeding

1. Origins

In the 1957 Treaty of Rome establishing the European Economic Community, the creation of a single market for intra-Community transport was judged as one of the necessary conditions for achieving the 'four freedoms' (Erdmenger, 1981). The mission is to ensure that transport policies are designed for the benefit of all sectors of society, businesses, cities and rural areas. Arts 74-84 of the Treaty of Rome form the legal basis of the common transport policy, which has been subsequently amended and shifted towards more regulatory measures, the most significant being the Single European Act in 1986 and the Treaty of the European Union in 1992. The Treaty of Amsterdam, in 1999, led to a further reinforcement of environment provisions in the transport sector and further strengthened the European Parliament's role in the co-decision process.

In terms of the external dimension of transport policy, the judgement by the European Court of Justice on AETR (European Agreement concerning the work of crews of vehicles engaged in international road transport) is important. It reads that the member states are no longer free to negotiate with others on an equal basis as autonomous sovereign states, but have to agree a common position within the Community and reach an understanding within the Council as to how much a position is to be pursued within a given negotiating forum, and by whom. Furthermore, the AETR judgement says that the Commission is in some cases entitled to make proposals and negotiate, while it is for the Council to conclude the agreement, which implies a measure of cooperation between the two institutions (shared competence). Nowadays these methods of cooperation are laid down in negotiating mandates agreed within the Council on a case-by-case basis.

On 12 September 2001, the Commission presented its White Paper on the future common transport policy. The 130-page document proposes 60 measures to overhaul the current transport policy in order to make it more sustainable and avoid huge economic losses due to congestion, pollution and accidents (Commission's formal right of initiative). The White Paper and its proposals constitute the first practical contribution to the sustainable development strategy adopted by the Gothenburg European Council in June 2001.

Generally speaking, transport is a response to a crisis-driven policy area. In terms of air transport, for example, the heavy losses suffered by Europe's leading airlines between 1990 and 1993 were not only because of the Gulf wars. In a climate of increasingly fierce international competition, airlines continued their restructuring in order to improve their productivity. In maritime policy, a number of stricter EC measures were deemed necessary in the aftermath of major shipping accidents such as those involving the Amoco Cadiz, the Exxon Valdez and the Herald of Free Enterprise. In particular member states such as the United Kingdom, France, Spain, Sweden and Germany, which were directly concerned, subsequently pushed for stricter regulations. The grounding of the tankers Braer, Aegean Sea and Estonia led to a common policy on safe sea – a package of some eight separate directives – not to mention the well-known Erika packages I, II and III pushed for by the Council and Spain and France in particular.

2. Main Council bodies involved

For the transport area a typical three-level approach holds true: Working groups, Coreper I and the Transport, Telecommunications and Energy Council, which meets with transport ministers when this issue is on the agenda. There are four working parties on transport questions: Working Party on Land Transport (H.1), Working Party on Shipping (H.2), Working Party on Aviation (H.3) and Working Party on Transport – Intermodal Questions and Networks (H.4) which meet about once every two weeks. The Council of transport ministers meets four times a year. In exceptional cases, the working group system is substituted by exploratory discussions among the presidency, the Secretariat of the Council of the European Union and the individual member state. As for the procedure on the Financial Perspectives in the European Council, the presidency might decide to opt for one-to-one exploratory discussions with the national delegations when the issue at stake is very ideologically driven as, for example, in the case of the Eurovignette Directive.

3. Applicable policy-making procedures

Co-decision is the procedure most often used in the area of transport policy. It applies, for example, for common rules on conditions under which non-resident carriers may operate transport and services within a member state, safety and other appropriate provisions (Article 71(1), ex Article 75).

Provisions concerning the principles of the regulatory system for transport, the application of which would be liable to have a serious effect on the standard of living and on employment in certain areas, and those on the operation of transport facilities (Article 71(2), ex Article 75), fall under the consultation procedure. Rules to abolish discrimination, which take the form of carriers charging different rates and imposing different conditions (Article 75, ex Article 79), are adopted by the Council acting by a qualified majority. Deciding whether, to what extent and by what procedure appropriate provisions may be laid down for sea and air transport (Article 80, ex Article 84) the Council acts by a qualified majority.

Community competence is not exclusive in such areas as aviation where member states share competence with the EC, so-called shared or 'mixed competence'. The 'open skies' judgments of 5 November 2002, for example, have given the Commission 'horizontal mandate' to negotiate with third countries by resolving the question of shared competence between the member states and the Community. In practice, member states often cede their negotiating role to the EC negotiator, and the European Commission negotiates. The Commission therefore attends negotiations on behalf of the EC and its member states. The procedure for concluding an agreement with one or more states or international organisations (Article 24) starts with the Council, which, when acting unanimously, may authorise the presidency or the Commission to open negotiations. Any agreement is then concluded by the Council acting unanimously.

4. Principal parties involved in developing the policy: Background and level of seniority

The normal procedure is for the Commission's proposals to be submitted for consideration by one of the working groups on transport matters. Since the first meetings are often devoted to very technical issues of the Commission's proposal, member states´ experts sent by their national capitals attend the first rounds of working group meetings. Later on, negotiations are taken over by the regular middle-ranking officials attached to the permanent representations of the member states. Gradually, over a succession of meetings, the differences may be refined and whittled down to a few key issues – for example a debate between those favouring increased liberalisation and those demanding more harmonisation of competitive conditions – or important national considerations such as the protection of lifeline services to isolated communities (Stevens, 2004: 76). These in turn may be further refined and reduced in Coreper I before the dossier goes to the Council itself, where ministers may succeed in bridging the remaining differences in views, or alternatively may fail to do so and return the dossier to Coreper and if necessary to the transport working group for further consideration.

It is worth highlighting here the role played by expert groups in the policy formulation phase and that of the comitology committees in the implementation phase. In transport, sixty-six expert groups were established by the Commission to help in the formulation of policy proposals. They also monitor whether or not competences are being overstepped. There are three consultative and scientific groups which have been formally established by a Commission Decision; twenty-seven permanent groups, the creation of which has been authorised by the Commission for a duration of more than five years and thirty-six temporary groups, the creation of which has been authorised by the Commission for a duration of less than five years. The comitology committees are involved in implementing legislative acts. In 2004, for transport, there were eighteen comitology committees, ranging from the 'Committee on application of the legislation on the minimum requirements for vessels bound for or leaving Community ports and carrying dangerous or polluting goods', through to the 'Committee on driving licences' to the 'Advisory Committee on unfair pricing practices in maritime transport'.

5. Consultation and approval processes

When a proposal has finally been adopted by the Commission and falls under co-decision, the European Parliament in general and its transport committee in particular can formally veto the legislative draft.

Since EU transport policies are, despite the qualified majority voting in some areas, agreed upon mostly unanimously, it is especially the big member states that can form blocking minorities with the help of other member states by calling on favours. Whereas the United Kingdom supported Germany on national weekend bans on lorries, it was Germany which endorsed the UK's position on the EU/US open skies agreements.

Furthermore, the preparation and implementation of EU transport policy by the Commission rely increasingly on expert advice. Expert groups made up of national and/or private-sector experts set up by the Commission provide it with specialist advice. They advise the Commission and its services on the preparation of legislative proposals and policy initiatives. The comitology committees deliver opinions on draft implementing measures submitted to them by the Commission pursuant to the basic legislative instrument and intervene within the framework of the advisory, the management and the regulatory procedure provided for that purpose.

In addition, the Commission's draft text is sent to the Economic and Social Committee (ECOSOC) and to the Committee of the Regions (COR). However, their role is advisory, with little direct impact on the outcome.

6. Development policy related input into the procedure

The move to integrate development policy considerations into transport policy has not gained much momentum yet. At the moment, there are only initiatives, which are part of the Barcelona process, promoting cooperation with the countries of the southern Mediterranean to improve transport infrastructure and alert the public and private players concerned. Whereas safety and security issues became important in the Commission's negotiations on an aviation agreement with Morocco, it is rather EU transport goals that influence development assistance: EU transport policy is 'exported' into the development sector. China, for example, received financial assistance to develop its aviation sector. Recently, however, member states and the Commission have become keen on linking the assistance closer to EU transport goals by requiring regulatory convergence from China.

7. Strengthening the process to secure a better development input

An important finding is that the effects of EU transport policy on the development process and vice versa are far less visible and identifiable compared to other policy areas. As the relationship between EU domestic transport policies and reaching the MDGs (Millennium Development Goals) in developing countries does not appear to be problematic, it is difficult to envisage institutional changes to strengthen development inputs in the policy-making process on domestic EU legislation. However there might be issues that are less visible or issues that come up in the future and in that case development experts would need to be involved.

Moreover, the technical knowledge and regulatory framework in place in the EU could contain lessons for infrastructure projects and transport policies in developing countries. Development specialists could consider building stronger contacts with the relevant European transport specialists in other to ensure their expertise can be used for EU development policy.

Overall it might be helpful to start with the role played by expert groups and comitology committees. Formally, their role is limited to either the policy formulation stage or the implementation stage. Informally, however, the Commission is advised by expert groups and comitology committees over the entire policy-making cycle. Here, the input of development specialists next to transport experts could help to frame Policy Coherence for Development (PCD) issues in terms of relevance for the transport sector.

8. Organigram of Transport Policy-Making in the Council of European Union

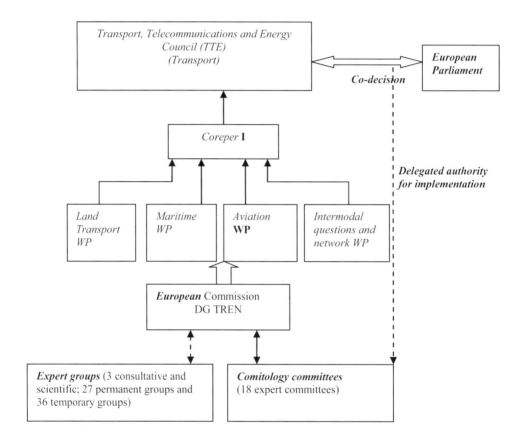

12. Fiche on EU Energy Policy

Louise van Schaik

1. Origins

The EU Treaty does not assign an explicit horizontal EU competence in the area of energy.[1] For almost 30 years, EU energy policy has in principle been confined to the narrow field of nuclear energy and coal based on the European Coal and Steel Community (ECSC) and the European Atomic Community (Euratom). Periodic attempts to extend the EU's jurisdiction to affect the choice of energy supply remained largely unsuccessful, since a majority of member states were not willing to give up real or perceived authority over the economically important issue of energy. Nevertheless, there have been a series of broad horizontal goals, such as promoting the rational use of energy, championing renewable energy, reducing Europe's dependency on oil import and notably liberalising energy markets. The policies were justified on the basis of internal market, competitiveness, environment or other EC competences and in general were politically acceptable when supported unanimously by all EU member states or at least by a qualified majority.[2]

Recently the draft Constitutional Treaty proposed to include an energy chapter, which merely resembles the current situation and stops short of providing the EU with any real power on the core issues of energy policy, namely member state energy choices, such choosing between nuclear, coal or gas and ultimately security of supply. In the absence of real EU power in energy policy, EU energy policy orientations will continue to rely on competencies other than energy, notably internal market and the environment. This is reflected in current EU energy policy priorities:

---

[1] For an overview of EU energy policy and competences, see Egenhofer (2001) available at http://www.ceps.be/Article.php?article_id=14

[2] Also article 3§1(u) of the TEC on activities of the Communities (within the context of its tasks/goals as defined in art. 2) includes a reference to "measures in the field of energy".

completion of the internal market in electricity and gas and the promotion of energy efficiency and renewables.

2. Main Council bodies involved

The leading Council formation on energy issues is the Transport, Telecommunications and Energy (TTE) Council, which is composed of ministers covering energy when this is the agenda item being discussed. Moreover, as a combined result of rapidly increased oil prices, the forecasted growth in import dependency on oil and gas and an increased importance attached to the climate change problem, energy has rapidly gained political momentum at the highest political level. It was discussed by the European heads of state and government in an informal summit at Hampton Court in the autumn of 2005 and in the Spring European Council in 2006 (on the basis of a green paper prepared by the Commission[3]). They decided to launch an *Energy Policy for Europe* with competitiveness, security of supply and environmental sustainability as its main themes. Because energy was on the agenda of the European Council, other Council formations also discussed energy issues as far as they were relevant in order to provide input, including the GAERC (security of supply, Russia, external relations and development issues), ECOFIN (energy markets), Competitiveness and Agriculture Council (biofuels).

In general, however, the European Council becomes only involved in highly political and strategic issues or in cross-border issues such as the Lisbon and Sustainable Development Strategies. On energy it has occasionally also been involved on liberalisation of electricity and gas markets. The March 2006 discussion on energy can therefore be considered quite exceptional, although it is likely to be continued in the future, as energy and particularly security of supply, are likely to remain issues high on the political agenda.

In order to prepare TTE Council meetings, energy issues are first of all discussed by the Working Party on Energy, which meets about once a week. There is also a High-Level WP on Energy, but this group seldom meets and in fact is actually the same as the energy WP, but with different

---

[3] A European Strategy for Sustainable, Competitive and Secure Energy, Green Paper.

participants (see section 4). It convened last in London, following the Hampton Court Summit. The issue of nuclear energy is covered in a separate Working Party on Atomic Questions with an Ad Hoc WP on Nuclear Safety, as well as in the Joint Working Party on Research/Atomic Questions.

Sometimes energy-related topics are discussed as well in other WPs, notably research, agriculture (biofuels), environment (climate change), competitiveness and growth and the political and security committee (security of supply, geopolitical energy issues). CODEV has been involved with regard to formulating the Council Conclusions on "integrating energy interventions into development cooperation" that were adopted by the GAERC on 10 April 2006 (see also point 6). Although energy issues are thus discussed in several WPs, when it comes to core energy issues for the EU internal market and energy legislation, the WP on energy is clearly in the lead.

Coreper I functions as the clearing house between the WP on Energy and the Council. Coreper II is involved with foreign policy, development and nuclear issues, which are decided upon by the GAERC formation of the Council of Ministers.

3. Applicable policy-making procedures

The competence areas on which energy policies are usually based such as internal market and environment are generally subject to the co-decision procedure with QMV used as the voting rule in the Council. EC Treaty articles on which energy legislation is based include 175 (environment), 95 (internal market), 156 (trans-European networks) and 133 (external action). Concerning energy, there are some important exceptions enshrined in the Treaty. For instance, Art. 175 stipulates that "measures significantly affecting a Member State's choice between different energy sources and the general structure of its energy supply" are subject to the consultation procedure with unanimity. Usually policy proposals are framed in such a way by the European Commission that this exception to co-decision does not apply.

For nuclear energy, the Euratom Treaty provisions apply, meaning that the vast majority of decisions are taken by unanimity. The EP is usually consulted, but there is no obligation to do so, implying that the EP cannot hold up decision-making by delaying its opinion, which theoretically it could do under the normal consultation procedure that applies under the TEC.

Bilateral and international relations on energy are either a shared competence between the EC and the EU member states or have remained within the domain of the member states (e.g. with regard to choices of their energy mix). In international fora where the EU acts in concert (e.g. the EU Energy Dialogue with Russia, the EU-OPEC Dialogue, the Energy Charter Treaty), either the Commission or the presidency is the EU's main representative speaking on behalf of the EC and the member states. It operates on the basis of what has been agreed upon in the Council or in EU coordination meetings in which the representatives of the member states and the Commission participate.

4. Principal parties involved in developing the policy: Background and level of seniority

Proposals for energy legislation are drafted by the European Commission, where DG TREN has the lead. Also other services follow energy dossiers closely, such as DG Environment, ENTREPRISE, SANCO, ECOFIN, and Competition. For implementation issues there are several comitology committees, such as the cross-border electricity committee. Perhaps more important is the role of the advisory committee of European Energy Regulators, ERGEG, which is composed of national energy regulators. In a different setting, but composed of the same people, the Council of European Energy Regulators (CEER) is taking care of stakeholder consultations with affected industry and other organizations, providing substantial input on technical energy issues (e.g. interconnection of the grid).

There are also more informal events where Commission officials, member states' representatives, industry and NGOs meet, such as the Florence (electricity), Madrid (gas) and Amsterdam (sustainable energy) Fora.

The participants in the Council WP on Energy are energy attachés from the Permanent Representations usually second by a national expert working for the Ministry in the home country. The participants of the High-level group are senior energy officials of the EU member states based in their home country (energy directors). The Atomic Questions and Nuclear Safety WPs are also staffed by attaches from the Permanent

Representations. They meet less often, the atomic questions about every two to three weeks and the nuclear safety WP only when relevant issues are at hand.

In most of the other WPs where energy issues are occasionally discussed the permanent representations are also in the lead staffing, but especially with regard to international issues it can also be the case that officials from national Ministries are the main representatives, as external representation is a sensitive issue for the EU member states touching upon their statehood and sovereignty.

In the European Parliament the Committee on Industry, Research and Energy is in the lead, with other committees following the work depending on the issue at stake (e.g. environment committee, foreign affairs committees).

With regard to sensitive pieces of energy legislation Presidencies have at times delayed or accelerated decision-making. As is highlighted under point 7 respective Presidencies have especially played a large role in putting the energy-development interface on the agenda.

The support of member states policies for energy policies is diverse and relates to their energy mix, energy import dependency and on whether energy is seen primarily as a tradable commodity for liberalised markets or as a product or service where state interventions should play a role. These differences also underlie problems encountered with the implementation of the internal energy market in the EU member states as is most clearly illustrated by the current energy sector enquiry by the Competition authority of the EU and the infringement procedures started up by DG TREN towards several Member States regarding insufficient implementation of EU energy regulations.

5. Consultation and approval processes

Energy has been a sensitive issue for cooperation between the EU member states. There are differences in interests between energy producers and non-producer countries, as well as different structures of national energy sectors. Member states are moreover foremost concerned about their own security of supply position, i.e. that there is enough energy for their country. The sensitivities are perhaps most clearly illustrated when discussions on energy competences in the light of Treaty revisions are taking place. Another consequence is that thus far new EU energy policy initiatives have been driven by the Commission, which has exploited institutional rules to take the initiative, to redefine the energy sector to the internal market, environmental policy and foreign policy (Andersen, 2000).

6. Development policy input into the procedure

A reliable and affordable energy supply is far from commonplace in the developing world, where over 2 billion people rely on biomass (wood, waste, etc.) as their primary energy source and 1.6 billion lack access to electricity[4]. Affordable energy is obviously an important condition for economic development. The current high prices of oil are having larger effects on developing countries with comparatively weak economies and often high losses in power production, transmission and distribution as well as in transportation and different end-uses of energy. To a certain extent they moreover compete with the EU and other energy importers for conventional energy sources and therefore it seems in the interest of all to improve energy efficiency, renewable energy and local energy systems in developing countries. It is important for the EU to ensure that new energy investments both in OECD and in developing countries are clean in order to achieve the drastic cuts in greenhouse gas emissions that are projected to be needed to reach the EU's climate change objectives.

A special case rises with developing countries where energy is produced. Although revenues from oil, gas and minerals in these countries could be very well used to foster economic growth and to reduce poverty this requires adequate governance systems which are often not in place or corrupted. This issue is addressed in particular by the Extractive Industries Transparency Initiative, which is supported amongst others by France and the UK and aims to improve transparency and accountability over revenue allocation.

Recent years have witnessed a remarkable increase in the attention paid to energy issues in EU development policy. The overall framework for this attention has been provided by the EU Energy Initiative (EUEI) that was launched at the World Summit for Sustainable Development organised in Johannesburg in 2002. Its progress was catalysed by a Commission Communication published in 2004 (711) and by Conclusions of the GAERC

---

[4] Communication (2005) on Sustainable Development strategy.

(8566/04). In order to ensure ownership and effectiveness in implementation, an extensive dialogue with the ACP countries was set up to consider the definite shape of the EUEI. The Energy Facility is funded from the 9th European Development Fund (conditionally). It is accompanied by a structure (modelled after the Water Initiative) in which member states coordinate their activities and financial investments on energy in developing countries. The secretariat is hosted within DG Development.

Key decisions included the approval in June 2005 of a 220 million euro ACP-EU Energy Facility[5] and the priority to energy in policy documents such as the European Consensus on Development (2005) and the EU Strategy for Africa (2005). In April 2006 the GAERC moreover adopted Council Conclusions integrating energy interventions into development cooperation, which are to be used as a reference point for the EU in many international meetings that will discuss energy and development; notably the ones taking place in the UN Commission on Sustainable Development (CSD), where energy is the key issue in 2006 and 2007. The Council Conclusions are based to a large extent on a senior officials seminar, organised by the Austrian presidency on Energy in the Context of Development Cooperation[6]. The seminar participants looked forward to upcoming international meetings where energy and development are on the agenda and took stock of the discussions in many meetings, seminars, conferences[7], organised internationally and in the EU, and notably referred back to the WSSD in Johannesburg in 2002, that still sets the main political framework for EU cooperation with developing countries on energy issues. An important driver for the EU's activities

---

[5] In addition to these resources, some of the 250 million euro allocated to energy efficiency and renewable energy projects within the context of the Intelligent Energy for Europe programme go to projects in developing countries.

[6] See for further information: http://www.ada.gv.at/view.php3?f_id=8969&LNG=en&version=

[7] E.g. the renewable energy conferences organised in Beijing (2005) and Bonn (2004), the Energy for Development Conference organised under the Dutch presidency (2004), the G-8 discussions on climate change and Africa (2005), the UNFCCC conference in Montreal (2005), the international energy technology cooperation initiatives, etc, etc.

"back then" has been the Commissions Communication "Energy cooperation with developing countries, published in 2002. The Council conclusions, as adopted in the GAERC, were prepared by CODEV.

The ACP-EU Energy Facility is part of the EU Energy Initiative. The Energy Facility is funded from the 9th European Development Fund, and a first call for projects was launched in June 2006.

Most resources and activities for energy investments are still coming from national development agencies, the IFIs and multilateral development banks. Policies to ensure that these energy investments are in line with the EU's poverty reduction, energy security and sustainable development objectives are still rather piecemeal, but in progress. The IFIs increasingly seem to realise the importance the EU attaches to this issue. The Presidency Conclusions of March 2006 mention moreover explicitly that in order to facilitate the access of developing countries to sustainable energy and related technologies, synergies with international organizations, including IFIs, should be fully exploited.

7. Strengthening the process to secure a better development input

In order to achieve more policy coherence for development improved (national) coordination between national experts working on development, energy, international finance, environment and foreign policy is essential. The recent processes towards an explicit and coherent EU position on energy and development cooperation seems to be a good example in this respect. It took several years of discussions, meetings and notably intensified efforts by the Commission and respective EU Presidencies, though, to get the relevant sectoral interests involved. And still many energy specialists do not consider development cooperation as an issue of their concern. One could also wonder whether they should, given the limited impact of EU internal energy legislation on development cooperation.

The internal side only matters indirectly as it influences the total amount of energy the EU is consuming from the world markets. Measures to increase energy efficiency and domestic energy production, notably by increasing the production of electricity from coal based in the EU, nuclear and renewable energy, diminish the energy demand and therefore could decrease the energy price for developing countries.

However, perhaps the international side is indeed more relevant and of more direct influence. It includes the UN Commission on Sustainable Development (CSD), which will focus on energy issues in 2006 and 2007, the upcoming St. Petersburg Summit of the G-8, where energy is the key agenda item, meetings of the IFIs and multilateral development banks affecting conditions for grants and loans for energy investments in developing countries, the post-2012 climate negotiations taking place in the context of the UNFCCC, and negotiations on standards of expert credit agencies (financial guarantee to many FDI flows targeted towards the energy sector), as taking place in the OECD.

It is essential that there is broader coordination between the above-mentioned sectoral interests to prepare for these meetings and to set clear policy priorities on energy in relationship to development cooperation. As the developments towards the April 2006 Council conclusions demonstrate, this does not necessarily have to take place in Council WP meetings, where important matters as internal EU legislation, etc are also on the agenda. The debate could indeed receive continued attention in the form of targeted informal initiatives (e.g. conferences, seminars), for instance initiated by the Commission or respective EU Presidencies; as occurred during the Dutch and Austrian presidencies. A potential topic for a future initiative could be biofuels, undoubtedly an issue covered in many international discussions. Another topic could be the development perspective on the EU energy White Paper that is due at the end of 2006. Finally, an issue where continuing coordination between member states' and Community efforts would seem worthwhile is the financing of energy investment in developing countries, where already a good start is being made in the context of the EU Energy Initiative.

8. Organigram of Energy Policy-Making in the European Union with a focus on the Council

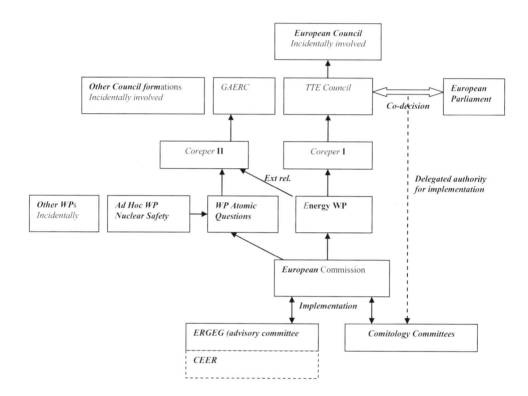

References and Further Reading

Allin, Dana, Michael Emerson, Marc Houben, François Heisbourg and Marius Vahl (eds) (2001-2006), *Readings in European Security*, Volumes 1-4, CEPS/IISS, Brussels and London.

Amnesty International, International Action Network on Small Arms (IANSA) and Oxfam (2004), *Guns or growth? Assessing the impact of arms sales on sustainable development*, Amnesty International, New York; IANSA; London and Oxfam, Oxford.

Andersen, Svein S. (2000), *EU Energy Policy: Interest Interaction and Supranational Authority*, ARENA Working Papers WP 00/5, Centre for European Studies, University of Oslo, Oslo.

Ashhoff, Guido (1999), "The coherence of policies towards developing countries: The case of Germany", in J. Forster and O. Stokke (eds), *Policy Coherence in Development Cooperation*, EADI Book Series 22 (European Association of Development Research and Training Institutes), London: Frank Cass.

Ashoff, Guido (2005), *Enhancing Policy Coherence for Development: Justification, Recognition and Approaches to Achievement*, German Development Institute, Bonn.

Balzacq, T. and S. Carrera (2005), *Migration, Borders and Asylum: Trends and Vulnerabilities in EU Policy*, CEPS Paperback, CEPS, Brussels.

Banchoff, T. (2002), "Institutions, Inertia and European Union Research Policy", *Journal of Common Market Studies*, Vol. 40, No. 1, pp. 1-21.

Beyers, J. and J. Trondall (2004), "How Nation States 'Hit' Europe: Ambiguity and Representation in the European Union", *West European Politics*, Vol. 27, No. 5, November, pp. 919-942.

Boswell, C., M-H Chou and J. Smith (2005), *Reconciling Demand for Labour Migration with Public Concerns about Immigration: The cases of Germany and the UK*, Anglo-German Foundation, London.

Coffey, Claire, Nikki Sporrong and Kate Bevins (2002), *Fisheries agreements with third countries – Is the EU moving towards sustainable development?*, Institute for European Environmental Policy, London.

Daugbjerg, C. (1999), "Reforming the CAP: Policy networks and broader institutional structures", *Journal of Common Market Studies*, 37(3): 407-428.

Dehousse, R. (2003), "Comitology: Who watches the watchmen?", *Journal of European Public Policy*, 10(5): 798-813.

DFID (1997), "White Paper – Eliminating world poverty: A challenge for the 21st Century", UK Department for International Development (DFID), London.

DFID (2000), "White Paper – Eliminating world poverty: Making globalization work for the poor", UK Department for International Development (DFID), London.

DFID (2003), *Promoting Institutional and Organisational Development*, UK Department for International Development (DFID), London.

Drury, E. (2003), *A League of Gentlemen: Who really runs EU Trade Decision-Making?*, WWF European Policy Office, WWF-UK, London, November.

DTI and DFID (2005), *Economic Partnership Agreements: Making EPAs wok for development*, UK Department of Trade and Industry and UK Department for International Development, London, March.

Dutzler, B. (2002), "Representation of the EU and the Member States in International Organisations", in S. Griller and B. Weidel (eds), *External economic relations and foreign policy in the European Union*, Vienna: Springer, pp. 153-189.

Eeckhout, P. (2004), *External Relations of the European Union*, Oxford: Oxford University Press.

Eeckhout, P. (2005), *External Relations of the European Union – Legal and Constitutional Foundations*, Oxford EC Law Library, Oxford: Oxford University Press.

Egeberg, M., G.F. Schaefern and J. Trondal (2003), "The many faces of EU committee governance", *West European Politics*, 26(3): 19-40.

Egeberg, M. (2005), *Executive Politics as Usual: Role Behaviour and Conflict Dimensions in the College of European Commissioners*, ARENA Working Paper No. 17, May, Centre for European Studies, University of Oslo, Oslo.

Egenhofer, C. (2001), *European Energy Policy at a Turning Point – An independent review of UK energy policy*, British Energy (available at http://www.ceps.be/Article.php?article_id=14).

Egenhofer, C. and K. Gialoglou (2004), *Rethinking the EU Regulatory Strategy for the Internal Energy Market*, CEPS Task Force Report No. 52, CEPS, Brussels, November.

Emerson, M. (2005), *What values for Europe? The Ten Commandments*, CEPS Policy Brief No. 65, CEPS, Brussels, February.

Erdmenger, Jürgen (1981), *EG unterwegs – Wege zur Gemeinsamen Verkehrspolitik*, Baden-Baden: Nomos Verlagsgesellschaft.

ECDPM & ICEI (2005), *EU mechanisms that promote policy coherence for development. Scoping study*, European Centre for Development Policy Management (ECDPM) and Instituto Complutense de Estudios Internacionales (ICEI), Maastricht and Madrid.

Falkner, Gerda (2003), "The EU's social dimension", in Michelle Cini (ed.), *European Union Politics*, Oxford: Oxford University Press, pp. 264-277.

Fouilleux, E., J. de Maillard and A. Smith (2005), "Technical or political? The working groups of the EU Council of Ministers", *Journal of European Public Policy*, 12,4: 609-623.

German Development Institute (GDI) (2005), *Between protectionism, poverty orientation and market efficiency: Reform of the EU sugar market organisation*, Briefing Paper, GDI, Bonn.

Häge, Frank (2006), *Who Decides in the Council of the European Union*, Working Paper, Leiden University.

Hayes-Renshaw, F. and H. Wallace (1997), *The Council of Ministers*, New York: St. Martin's Press.

Hayes-Renshaw, F., W. Van Aken and H. Wallace (2006), "When and Why the EU Council of Ministers Votes Explicitly", *Journal of Common Market Studies*, Volume 44, Number 1, pp. 161-94.

Hayes-Renshaw, F. and H. Wallace (2006), *The Council of Ministers* (2nd edition), Houndsmill, et al., Palgrave Macmillan.

Hervey, Tamara (1998), *European Social Law and Policy*, London: Pearson.

Hill, C. and M. Smith (2005), *International Relations in the EU*, Oxford: Oxford University Press.

Hix, Simon (2005), *The political system of the European Union*, London: Palgrave.

Hoebink, P. (1999), "Coherence and development policy: The case of the European Union", in J. Forster and O. Stokke (eds), *Policy coherence in development cooperation*, EADI Book Series 22, London: Frank Cass.

Hoebink, P. (2005), *The Coherence of EU Policies: Perspectives from the North and the South*, study commissioned by the European Union's Poverty Reduction Effectiveness Programme, Brussels (see www.ec-prep.org).

Holland, Martin (2002), *The European Union and the Third World*, London: Palgrave.

House of Commons, International Development Committee (2005), "The Commission for Africa and Policy Coherence for Development: First do not harm" http://www.publications.parliament.uk/pa/cm200405/cmselect/cmintdev/123/123.pdf).

Kohler-Koch, B. and R. Eising (eds) (1999), *The Transformation of Governance in the European Union*, London: Routledge.

Lamin, M. (2004), "Climate change and development: The role of EU development cooperation", *IDS Bulletin*, 35,3: 62-64, Institute of Development Studies, University of Sussex, Brighton.

Larsson, Torbjörn (2003), *Pre-cooking – The World of Expert Groups*, ESO report, Expert Group on Public Finance, Swedish Ministry of Finance, Stockholm.

Lewis, Jeffrey (2003), "The Council of the European Union", in Michelle Cini (ed.), *European Union Politics*, Oxford: Oxford University Press, pp. 148-165.

LMC International (2004), "EU sugar reform: The implications for the development of LDCs", Oxford.

Lord, C. (2005), *A Democratic Audit of the European Union*, Houndsmill: Palgrave Macmillan.

Manners, I. (2002), "Normative Power Europe: A Contradiction in Terms?", *Journal of Common Market Studies*, 40(2): 235-258.

Meunier, S. and K. Nicolaidis (1999), "Who speaks for Europe? The Delegation of Trade Authority in the EU", *Journal of Common Market Studies*, September.

Meunier, S. and K. Nicolaidis (2005), "The European Union as a trade power", in C. Hill and M. Smith, *International Relations and the European Union*, Oxford: Oxford University Press.

Netherlands Organisation for International Cooperation in Higher Education (Nuffic) (2003), *Report of the expert meeting on migration, brain drain and development*, from the Nuffic meeting held 11 December, Scheveningen, , The Hague.

Nugent, Neill (1999), *The Government and Politics of the European Union* (4th edition), London: Palgrave.

Ochs, A. and M. Schaper (2004), "Conflict or Cooperation? Transatlantic Relations in the Environmental Field", paper presented at the 2005 Conference of the EU Studies Association (EUSA), Austin, TX, April.

OECD (1996), *Shaping the 21st Century. The Contribution of Development Co-operation*, OECD, Paris.

OECD (2001), *The DAC Guidelines on poverty reduction* (includes a checklist for policy coherence), OECD, Paris.

OECD (2003), *Policy coherence: Vital for global development*, Policy Brief, OECD, Paris, July.

OECD (2004), *A comparative analysis of institutional mechanisms to promote policy coherence for development*, OECD, Paris.

OECD (2005a), *Policy Coherence for Development: Promoting Institutional Good Practice*, OECD, Paris.

OECD (2005b), *Fostering Development in a Global Economy: A Whole of Government Perspective*, OECD, Paris.

OECD (2005c), *Agriculture and Development: The Case for Policy Coherence*, OECD, Paris.

OECD (2005d), *Migration, Remittances and Development*, OECD, Paris.

OECD (2005e), *Miracle, Crisis and Beyond: A Synthesis of Policy Coherence towards East Asia*, OECD, Paris.

OECD (2005f), *Fishing for Coherence: Fisheries and Development Policies*, OECD, Paris.

OECD (2005g), *Trade, Agriculture and Development: Policies Working Together*, OECD, Paris.

OECD (2005h), *Making Poverty Reduction Work*, OECD, Paris.

Opoku, C. and A. Jordan (2004), "Impact Assessment in the EU: A global sustainable development perspective", paper presented at the Conference on the Human Dimension of Global Environmental Change, Berlin, 3-4 December.

Peterson, J. (2001), "The choice for EU theorists: Establishing a common framework for analysis", *European Journal of Political Research*, 39: 289-318.

Peterson, J. and E. Bomberg (1999), *Decision-Making in the European Union*, Basingstoke: Macmillan.

Pocciotto, R. (2004), "Policy coherence and development evaluation. Concepts, issues and possible approaches", paper presented at the OECD policy workshop on Institutional Approaches to Policy Coherence for Development, Paris.

Puetter, U. (2004), "Governing informally: The role of the Eurogroup in EMU and the Stability and Growth Pact", *Journal of European Public Policy*, 11(5): 854-870.

Renda, A. (2006), *Impact Assessment in the EU – The State of the Art and the Art of the State*, CEPS Paperback, CEPS, Brussels.

Richardson, J. (2000), "Government, interest groups and policy change", *Political Studies*, 48(5): 1006-1025.

Roodman, D. (2004), *An Index of Donor Performance*, Working Paper No. 42, Center for Global Development, Washington, D.C.

Schmidt, S. (2004), "Eastward enlargement and EU development policy", *Osteuropa*, 54: 5-6.

Sherrington, Philippa (2000), *The Council of Ministers. Political Authority in the European Union*, London: Pinter.

Simon, Duke (2002), *The EU and Crisis Management: Developments and Prospects*, European Institute of Public Administration (EIPA), Maastricht.

Spence, David (2004), "Negotiating and Bargaining in the Council", in Martin Westlake and David Galloway (eds), *The Council of the European Union*, London: John Harper Publishing, pp. 233-324.

Stevens, Handley (2004), *Transport Policy in the European Union*, London: Palgrave Macmillan.

Tallberg, J. (2004), "The Power of the Presidency: Brokerage, Efficiency and Distribution in EU Negotiations", *Journal of Common Market Studies*, 42(5): 999-1022.

UK Parliament, House of Lords, European Union Committee (2005), *Too much or too little? Changes to the EU sugar regime*, London.

Van Eekelen, Willem (2006), *From Words to Deeds: The Continuing Debate on European Security*, CEPS Paperback, CEPS, Brussels and the Geneva Centre for Democratic Control of Armed Forces, Geneva.

Van Schaik, L. and C. Egenhofer (2005), *Improving the Climate – Will the new Constitution strengthen the EU's performance in international climate negotiations?*, CEPS Policy Brief No. 63, CEPS, Brussels, February.

Westlake, Martin and David Galloway (2004), *The Council of the European Union*, London: John Harper Publishing.

Woolcock, S. (2005), "Trade Policy from Uruguay to Doha and Beyond", in H. Wallace, W. Wallace and M.A. Pollack (eds), *Policy-Making in the European Union*, Oxford: Oxford University Press.

Official EU Documents

Council of the European Union (1994), *Recommendations to the European Council – Europe and the Global Information Society*, report prepared by the High-Level Group on the Information Society ('Bangemann Report'), 26 May.

Council of the European Union (2002), Modification of the terms of reference of the High-Level Working Group on Asylum and Migration (HLWG), 9433/02, Brussels, 30.5.2002.

Council of the European Union (2003), Draft Council Conclusions on Migration and Development, 8927/03, Brussels.

Council of the European Union (2003), Decision 2003/840/EC of 17 November 2003 relating to the conclusion on behalf of the European Community of Council of Europe Convention No. 180 on information and legal cooperation on information society services, OJ L 321, 06.12.2003.

Council of the European Union (2004), Directive 2004/114/EC of 13 December 2004 on the conditions of admission of third-country nationals for the purposes of studies, pupil exchanges, unremunerated training or voluntary service, OJ L 375, 23.12.2004.

Council of the European Union (2004), Decision 2004/927/EC of 22 December 2004 providing for certain areas covered by Title IV of Part Three of the Treaty establishing the European Community to be governed by the procedure set out in Art. 251 of that Treaty, OJ L 396/45, 31.12.2004.

Council of the European Union (2005), Council Conclusions on Policy Coherence for Development (included in the Conclusions on the Millennium Development Goals), 24 May.

Council of the European Union (2005), The Hague Programme: Strengthening Freedom, Security and Justice in the European Union, 2005/C53/01, OJ C 53/1, 3.3.2005.

Council of the European Union (2005), Recommendation 2005/762/EC of 12 October 2005 to facilitate the admission of third-country nationals to carry out scientific research in the European Community, OJ L 289/26, 3.11.2005.

Council of the European Union (2005), List of Council Preparatory Bodies, 15180/05, Brussels, 5.12.2005.

Council of the European Union (2005), Draft Council Conclusions on Migration and External Relations, 14310/05, Brussels.

Council of the European Union (2005), Press Release from the 2691ˢᵗ Council Meeting, General Affairs and External Relations, Brussels, 21-22 November 2005, 14172/05 (Presse 289), Brussels, 21.11.2005.

Council of the European Union (2005), *Seventh Annual Report according to Operative Provision 8 of the European Union Code of Conduct on Arms Exports,* 14053/05, Brussels, 17.11.2005.

Council of the European Union (2006), Council Conclusions on the EU Aid Effectiveness Package, b: Policy coherence for development: working programme 2006-2007, Press Release 2723ʳᵈ Council meeting, 7939/06.

Council of the European Union (2006), Conclusions from the General Affairs and External Relations Council meeting on an EU strategy for action on the crisis in human resources for health in developing countries, Luxembourg, 10.4.2006.

Council of the European Union (2006), *User's Guide to the EU Code of Conduct on Arms Exports*, 5179/1/06 Rev. 1, PESC 18, COARM 1, Brussels, 19.4.2006.

European Commission (1987), *Towards a Dynamic European Economy, Green Paper on the Development of the Common Market for Telecommunications Services and Equipment*, COM(87) 290, Brussels, June.

European Commission (1994), Communication on Europe's Way to the Information Society – An Action Plan, COM(94) 347 final, Brussels, 10.7.1994.

European Commission (2000), Rules of Procedure of the Commission, COM(2000) 3614 final, in OJ L 308/26 of 8.12.2000, Brussels.

European Commission (2000), Communication on a Community Immigration Policy, COM(2000) 757 final, Brussels, 22.11.2000.

European Commission (2001), Green paper on the future of the Common Fisheries Policy, COM(2001) 135 final, Brussels, 20.3.2001.

European Commission (2001), Proposal for a Council Directive on the conditions of entry and residence of third-country nationals for the purpose of paid employment and self-employed economic activities, COM(2001) 386 final, Brussels, 11.7.2001.

European Commission (2001), Communication on the International Dimension of the European Research Area, COM(2001) 346 final, Brussels, 25.06.2001.

European Commission (2002), Communication from the Commission on Impact assessment, COM(2002) 276 final, Brussels, 5.6.2002.

European Commission (2002), Communication on Integrating Migration Issues in the European Union's Relations with Third Countries, COM(2002) 703 final, Brussels, 3.12.2002.

European Commission (2004), Communication on Challenges for the European Information Society beyond 2005, COM(2004) 757 final, Brussels, 19.11.2004.

European Commission (2005), Communication on a Policy Plan on Legal Migration, COM(2005), 669 final, Brussels, 21.12.2005.

European Commission (2005), Communication on Migration and Development: Some Concrete Orientations, COM(2005) 390 final, Brussels, 1.9.2005.

European Commission (2005), Communication on a European Programme for Action to Confront HIV/AIDS, Malaria and Tuberculosis through External Action, COM(2005) 179 final, Brussels, 27.4.2005.

European Commission (2005), Communication on an EU Strategy for Africa: Towards a Euro-African Pact to Accelerate Africa's Development, COM(2005) 489 final, Brussels, 12.10.2005.

European Commission (2005), *The trade and development aspects of EPA negotiations*, Commission Staff Working Document, 9 November, SEC (2005) 1459.

European Commission (2005), Communication on an EU Strategy for Action on the Crisis in Human Resources for Health in Developing Countries, COM(2005) 642 final, Brussels, 12.12.2005.

European Commission (2005), Communication on i2010 – A European Information Society for Growth and Employment, COM(2005) 229 final, Brussels, 31.5.2005.

European Commission (2005), Communication from the Commission to the Council, the European Parliament and the European Economic and Social Committee of 12 April 2005 on Policy coherence for development – Accelerating progress towards attaining the Millennium Development Goals.

European Commission, *Financing ICT for Development: The EU approach* (http://www.dfid.gov.uk/pubs/files/eu-financ-wsis-english.pdf).

European Commission (2006), *Policy Coherence for Development. Work Programme 2006-2007*, Commission Staff Working Paper, European Commission, Brussels.

European Council (1999), Presidency Conclusions of the Tampere European Council of 15-16 October, SN 200/1/99, Brussels.

European Council (2002), Presidency Conclusions of the Seville European Council of 21-22 June, SN 13463/02, Brussels, 24.10.2002.

European Council (2003), Presidency Conclusions of the Thessaloniki European Council of 19-20 June 2003, SN11638/03, Brussels, 1.10.2003.

European Parliament (2005), *Report on the Council's Sixth Annual Report according to Operative Provision 8 of the European Union Code of Conduct on Arms Exports*, Rapporteur: Raül Romeva i Rueda, A6-0292/2005 final, 12.10.2005.

European Parliament (2006), Report on the development impact of Economic Partnership Agreements, European Parliament Committee on Development, 1 March, A6-0053/2006.

European Parliament (2006), *Report on the Special Report from the European Ombudsman following the draft recommendation to the Council of the European in complaint 2395/2003/GG concerning the openness of the meetings of the Council when acting in its legislative capacity (2005/2243 (INI))*, Rapporteur: David Hammerstein Mintz, Session Document A6-0056/2006 final, 2.3.2006.

"Joint statement by the Council and the representatives of the governments of the Member States meeting within the Council, the European Parliament and the Commission on European Union Development Policy: The European Consensus" ('European Consensus on Development'), OJ C 46/01, Brussels, 24.2.2006.

Glossary of Abbreviations and Terms

@LIS	The Alliance for the Information Society, a partnership between Europe and Latin America to promote dialogue on regulatory issues, demonstration projects and connections between researchers and communities.
ACP	African, Caribbean and Pacific countries
AIDCO	Europe Aid Coordination Office
AmCham	American Chamber of Commerce
CAN	Climate Action Network
CAP	Common Agricultural Policy
CDM	Clean Development Mechanism (one of the flexible mechanisms of the Kyoto Protocol)
CFSP	Common foreign and security policy
CIA	Committee on Immigration and Asylum
CIREFI	Centre for Immigration, Discussion and Exchange on the Crossing of Frontiers and Immigration
CIVCOM	Committee for Civilian Aspects of Crisis Management
CMO	Common Market Organisation
COARM	Council Working Group on Conventional Arms Exports
COCON	Working group on consular services
Co-decision	Under the co-decision procedure (Art. 251 of the EC Treaty) the European Parliament and the Council jointly adopt instruments. The procedure comprises two readings.
CODEV	Council Working Party on Development Cooperation
COGEGA	General Confederation of Agricultural Co-operatives
CONUN	Working group on the United Nations
COPA	Committee of Professional Agricultural Organisations
COPS	Comité de politique et sécurité (Political and Security Committee in English)

COR	Committee of the Regions
Coreper (I & II)	Comité des représentants permanents [Committee of Permanent Representatives]; Coreper I consists of deputy heads of mission and deals largely with social and economic issues; Coreper II consists of heads of mission and focuses on political, financial and foreign policy issues
COTER	Council Working Group on Terrorism
Council (of Ministers)	Officially the Council of the EU, usually referred to as Council or Council of Ministers, consists of the portfolio ministers of the EU member states. The Council adopts laws, often in co-decision with the European Parliament.
CREST	EU Scientific and Technical Research Committee
CSD	Commission on Sustainable Development
DFID	Department for International Development
DG	Directorate General (of the European Commission)
DG AGRI	Directorate General for Agriculture and Rural Development
DG BUDGET	Directorate General for Budget
DG DEV	Directorate General for Development
DG ECFIN	Directorate General for Economic and Financial Affairs
DG ENV	Directorate General for Environment
DG FISH	Directorate General for Fisheries
DG INFSO	Directorate General for Information Society and Media
DG REGIO	Directorate General for Regional Policy
DG RELEX	Directorate General for External Relations
DG SANCO	Directorate General for Health and Consumer Protection
DG TRADE	Directorate General for Trade
EC	European Community, the pillar of the European Union in which the Community policies are placed. The EC has legal personality and falls under the jurisdiction of the European Court of Justice, i.e. EU "supreme court".
ECCA	European Cable Communications Association

ECCP	European Climate Change Programme
ECOFIN	Economic and Finance Council
ECOSOC	Economic and Social Committee
ECTA	European Competitive Telecommunications Associations
EDCTP	European and Developing Countries Clinical Trials Partnership
EDF	European Development Fund
EEA	European Economic Area (adds Norway, Liechtenstein and Iceland EU activities)
EES	European Employment Strategy
EFMA	European Fertilizer Manufacturing Association
EMCO	Employment Committee
EPSCO	Employment, Social Policy, Health and Consumer Affairs Council
ERA	European Research Area
ERDF	European Regional Development Fund
ERG	European Regulators Group
ERGEG	European Regulators Group for Electricity and Gas
ESDP	European security and defence policy
ESPRIT	European Strategic Programme for Research and Development in Information Technology
ETNO	European Telecommunications Network Operators' Association
EU	European Union, a *sui generis* polity, with intergovernmental and supranational characteristics. The EU is currently composed of 25 member states. Its activities are grouped in three pillars: the EC pillar, the CFSP pillar and the Justice and Home Affairs pillar.
EU Council	Officially the Council of the EU, also referred to as Council or Council of Ministers, consists of the portfolio ministers of the EU member states. The Council adopts laws, often in co-

	decision with the European Parliament.
EU ETS	EU Emissions Trading Scheme (for carbon dioxide of large industrial plants)
EUMC	EU Military Committee
EUMEDIS	Funding for the development of the Information Society in the Mediterranean area.
EUMS	EU Military Staff
European Commission	The EU's executive body, it proposes legislation, looks after implementation of legislation and is the guardian of the treaties. It is composed of 25 independent members, i.e. the European Commissioners, one from each EU member state.
European Council	Consists of the heads of government and state and the European Commission President. It meets four times a year to provide guidance on the day-to-day management of the EU and to take strategic decisions.
EUTC	European Trade Union Confederation
FP	Framework Programme (for Research)
FPA	Fisheries Partnership Agreement
GAERC	General Affairs and External Relations Council
GCIM	Global Commission on International Migration
HLWG	High-Level Working Group
HR	High Representative of the CFSP
ICC	International Chamber of Commerce
ICT	Information and Communications Technologies
IEI	International Environmental Issues
IFI	International Finance Institution
IGC	Intergovernmental Conference. Negotiations between the member state governments with a view to amending the treaties.
ILO	International Labour Organisation
INCO	International Scientific Cooperation

INTUG	International Telecommunications Users Group
IOM	International Organisation for Migration
IPCC	International Panel on Climate Change
IRG	Independent Regulators Group
ITRE	Industry, Trade, Research and Energy Committee (of the European Parliament)
JHA	Justice and Home Affairs
JI	Joint Implementation (one of the flexible mechanisms of the Kyoto Protocol)
LDC	Least Developed Countries
LUFPIG	Land use and Food Policy Intergroup
MEA	Multilateral Environmental Agreement
MEP	Member of the European Parliament
NGO	Non-governmental organisation
OMC	Open Method of Coordination
PMG	Political and Military Group
Presidency	The Presidency of the EU is held in turn on a six-monthly basis by each member state. The Presidency chairs the meetings of the European Council and Council of Ministers and represents the European Union externally in many international organisations.
PROCIV	Working group on rescue operations
PSC	Political and Security Committee
QMV	Qualified majority voting, indicates the number of votes required in the Council for a decision to be adopted. Member states' votes are weighted on the basis of their population and corrected in favour of less-populated countries. A proposal is accepted if it is supported by 71% of the votes and represents at least 62% of the population.
RELEX	Directorate-General for External Relations in the European Commission

RFO	Regional Fisheries Organisation
RTD	Research, Technology and Development
SANCO	Health & Consumer Protection Directorate General
SCA	Special Committee on Agriculture
SCIFA	Strategic Committee on Immigration, Frontiers and Asylum
SPC	Social Protection Committee
TCNs	Third country nationals
TEC	Treaty establishing the European Community
TENs	Trans-European Networks
TEU	Treaty on European Union
TREN	Directorate-General for Transport and Energy in the European Commission
TTE	Transport, Telecommunications and Energy
UN	United Nations
UNEP	United Nations Environment Programme
UNFCCC	United Nations Framework Convention on Climate Change
UNICE	Union of European Employers Associations
WBCSD	World Business Council for Sustainable Development
WP	Working Party
WSIS	World Summit on the Information Society
WWF	World Wildlife Fund for Nature
WWF	World Wildlife Fund